Dr. Hernández wrot goal of inspiring chi that they can achieve in life. He outlines his journey from growing up in a poor farming community in Mexico to becoming a surgeon with the skills to bring healing to many people. He gives credit and honor to the individuals that helped him in the formation of his character, drive, courage, and integrity.

I hope this book gets into the hands of many educators, parents, and others who work with children. May we model, encourage, and inspire children to believe and dream as did those adults in Dr. Hernández's life. It's the hope for our future.

—Robert Murillo, MD FAAP

This autobiography of Edgar Hernández takes you from his boyhood adventures with his grandfather in Mexico to the trials and tribulations of trying to enter the United States with his brother, Miguel. Edgar's commitment to pursuing his dreams, especially when confronted by a range of obstacles, is awe-inspiring. Young readers will enjoy the extraordinary adventures of Edgar, the courageous boy who never gave up on his dreams.

**—Molly Martin Valenzuela,
early childhood educator**

Throughout this book, my grandfather—Edgar Hernández—shares the story of how, as a young boy, he chased his dreams. The relentless courage he showed in both the most tragic and most exciting times is inspiring as well as the adult role models that guided him to where he is now. Not only does this book provide the message that children can achieve their big dreams, but it is also a great reminder for all the adults who may have forgotten those that have helped them accomplish their dreams. I hope whoever reads this sees how resilient children are and that they should never be underestimated. Additionally, I hope children see that they have the ability to achieve whatever they set their minds, to no matter what.

—Elisa Hernandez, MAS-MFT

Little Hands, Big Dreams is an incredible true story that showcases the life of the gifted storyteller and outstanding surgeon Dr. Edgar Hernández. As a child, Edgar's life was inspired and shaped by his grandfather, who took him on many adventures in their village in rural Mexico. His grandfather believed in him and his big dream to become a great surgeon. This book gives the story of how Edgar made that dream come true. Edgar's road to success was paved with belief, hard work, and love. I look forward to reading this book to my grandchildren for many years to come.

—Rebecca Rowley, retired elementary teacher (26 years) and reading specialist at Safford Unified School District, Safford, Arizona

Little Hands, Big Dreams

The Making of a Surgeon

Edgar H. Hernández, MD, MS, FACS

Little Hands, Big Dreams
The Making of a Surgeon

First Edition
First Printing 2025

ISBN: 979-8-9925638-0-1 (paperback)
ISBN: 979-8-9925638-1-8 (E-book)

Cover and interior design: JetLaunch.net

To all children who have dreams, may this book inspire and motivate you.

To all children who don't yet have dreams, may this book inspire and motivate you.

And to all grandparents, may you read this book to your grandchildren to inspire them to dream big.

Here is one of my favorite quotes from Walt Disney:

"All our dreams can come true if we have the courage to pursue them. If you can dream it, you can do it."

An Invitation

Dear Reader,

This book is an invitation for you to dream with me. In this book, I tell the story of how, as a child, I had big dreams in life and how I dared to chase those dreams. Through this book, let's walk together with curiosity and hope. Let's get in touch with the wonders of nature. Let's recognize the people we love. Let's celebrate life's joys and make note of life's hardships. Let's learn to voice our biggest dreams and then act with endurance to make those dreams come true. Travel with me on this journey of chasing big dreams, and when the book is complete, keep walking that journey. Chase your big dreams.

Edgar Hernandez, MD, MS, FACS
Tempe, AZ
February 24, 2025

Contents

Chapter 1

Lucky Hand

I was at the beach, pulling apart a coconut, when I felt a stinging sensation in my hand. Then almost immediately I noticed a tightness in my chest. Confused and afraid, I screamed out, "Abuelito! Abuelito!"

I could feel my body trembling and at the same time becoming rigid. My lips and feet felt as if they were getting attacked by bees. The burning sensation in my hand traveled up into my arm. It was pulsing and growing by the second.

The world outside me seemed to spin and jump in a cruel kind of dance. I looked up at the clouds. They seemed to be spiraling around me as if they wanted to pounce on me and beat me.

I managed to call again in a rushed but weak voice, "Abuelito! . . . Abuel—"

A distance from me I heard a man shout, "Andres! Your grandson needs help!"

I spotted my grandfather rushing towards me, his beard slanting left. His hat had fallen from his head and was hanging at his back from a string. I could see the machete on the left side of his hip, flap-flapping as he ran. He had a fearful look in his eyes.

Next, I felt the strength of his arms, lifting my stiff, doll-like body.

I slurred out, "Escorpión." Scorpion.

After that, I dropped into unconsciousness.

"Edgar, Edgar, mi hijo! Talk to me, talk to me, it's Abuelito. Can you hear me?" a voice beckoned me from my deep sleep.

It began to register—the voice of my beloved grandfather.

Next, I tasted saltwater on my lips, but I could not swallow. I noticed a stinging sensation in my hand and arm, but at the same time, the area felt numb.

I half opened my eyes—two, maybe even three, grandfathers stood before me as my eyes bounced around.

Then I heard a loud crash. A tremendous ocean wave had thrown itself onto the beach.

"Edgar, Edgar—wake up!"

With each of my hands, I dug into the wet sand that I found myself lying on. Looking up, I could make out my grandfather more clearly now.

"Look, Abuelito, look," I managed, pointing out to him my fists full of sand.

My grandfather looked to the sky, saying, "Thank you, Lord!"

He hugged me like never before.

Meanwhile, several men surrounded us. Their worried faces changed to smiles of relief. One of the men recommended to my grandfather, "Andres, you should bathe the boy in kerosene to kill the scorpion poison that entered his body. That's what we do in our village."

"Gracias, but I don't think it's necessary," my grandfather replied.

Another man confided to me, "Your grandfather is a brave man. There was only one thing he could think of when he grabbed you, and that was to take you to the ocean and place you in the water. You were sweating up a storm, and he wanted to get water on you to cool you down. You were thrashing about violently. It was horrific. So many children, just as young and small as you, die from scorpion bites, but—gracias a Dios—you survived."

I knew this man was telling the truth because I'd seen it myself. A few years earlier, I was walking with my father when we came upon a gathering of people at a small house. Inside, I saw a tiny wooden box sitting on a table. Men and women stood around it, weeping.

There was an old man playing the violin and chanting. The sounds were haunting. This is my earliest memory. It's one I'll never forget.

Yes, I was lucky that I survived and that my grandfather had been with me because it was not rare for scorpion stings to kill children in our area.

And so, I experienced early on the mystery, wonder, and danger of the natural world.

My name is Edgar Hernández. This is my story. Here, I tell where I come from and the people and places that shaped me. I share my dreams—the big dreams that I had as a child and all I did—plus the help I received—to make my dreams come true. Mine is the story of what it looks like when big dreams meet with belief, persistence, and an incredible group of supporters. Along the way, there are plenty of instances of beauty, wonder, and—of course—danger. After all, that's what we encounter when we chase big dreams.

> **In this chapter, Edgar faced a sudden crisis but had someone he trusted to help him. Who in your life encourages you to stay strong when things get difficult? How can you learn to stay calm and determined in tough situations?**

Chapter 2

By the Light of the Moon

I n 1950, I was born in La Mira, a small village in rural Mexico. La Mira sat by the Pacific Ocean and had two large rivers framing its sides. During the rainy season, these rivers could overflow and flood our village.

My grandfather told stories about past floods where people had to swim where we would now walk. Cattle, goats, chickens, horses, trees, homes, and even people were dragged away in the floodwaters.

One time, my grandfather and I saw men taking oxen across one of the rivers. The men found the narrowest spot, but it was still deep. They held onto the oxen's tails while the animals swam across!

In Spanish, the word for grandfather is abuelo. I called my grandfather either "Abuelo" or "Abuelito," which means "little grandfather." My grandfather was very wise. He could not read or write, but he knew everything about life. He knew all about the seasons. He could predict rain better than any weatherman. He considered the universe and nature his biggest partners in life.

One day, we went to his small farm located near a beach called Playa Azul. We were there to check on the watermelons. Though all the watermelons looked the same to me, he knew exactly which ones were ripe. I can still see him out in the field thumping watermelons.

"Abuelito, why are you thumping the watermelons?" I asked.

"Because it's going to tell me how sweet they are. When I hear a deep, hollow sound, I know the watermelon is no good. It's too ripe. I cut them when they're perfect and the sound is good."

Then he chose a watermelon, cut it from the vine, and brought it to me.

With his machete, he cut the watermelon in half. Its color was a perfect dark pink. He cut a piece and handed it to me.

I took a bite. It was cool, crisp, and sweet.

"Abuelito, why do you plant your watermelons in between rows of corn?" I asked.

He told me that the corn shaded the watermelons, and the watermelons helped the corn grow by putting nutrients in the soil. They were like good friends helping each other.

My grandfather awakened me early one morning, so we could set out on a special two-hour "trip of nature."

"Nature is always working, Edgar, and I want you to see it," he said.

With my hand in his, we started walking. His hand was thick, rough, and strong. He had muscular arms although he was thin. He had white hair, a white beard, and many wrinkles on his face. He was a farmer, so he was in the sun almost every day and his skin was tan. As was standard for the men in our small village of farmers, my grandfather wore a white shirt and white pants that tied at the waist with a cord. The clothes were made out of a strong, rough cotton material that was also used for making sacks that held grain, fruits, and vegetables. The kids in La Mira also wore clothes made of this white sackcloth material, so it was what I was wearing too.

On his head my grandfather wore a straw hat with a string tied at his neck. A machete strapped to his black belt hung at his left hip, parallel to his thigh—another feature of the men in our town.

I once asked my grandfather why he cleaned and sharpened his machete every evening. He responded, "I use this machete in many ways each day. Today I used it to trim hedgerows, cut down bunches of bananas, and slice open watermelons. For our good health, it should always be clean. Just like our hands and dishes."

As we walked along the ocean shore in the still dark early morning, we talked about everything, including oysters, clams, sharks, and all types of fish. He warned me to be careful when eating oysters because they can cause illness if they are not fresh and clean. My grandfather described various types of fish and how each one tasted different. He said that from a single taste usually he could determine exactly what type of fish it was.

He explained that the ocean's salty water helped skin problems heal quickly. My grandfather had a cut from his elbow to his wrist. He bathed it in salt water, and it healed beautifully.

My grandfather also talked about the sun. He didn't know the word "photosynthesis," but he knew how the sun gave life to everything.

"Edgar, you know how to keep me young with your endless curiosity and many questions," my grandfather often told me.

And it was true—I was a kid that asked many questions. "Why do we get old?" "Why do we have to die?

"Why do we get sick?" Sometimes people around me would become irritated, but not my grandfather.

As we walked, the moonlight shone around us. It was so bright that it made the ocean look like a glass surface. My grandfather explained how the shape of the moon could change things—when it would rain, when crops would grow, and even how people felt. "The moon holds us in its arms," he said.

He explained how the attitudes of human beings changed due to the shape of the moon. "When the moon is in crescent, people are extremely unpredictable. We avoid discussing business when the moon is crescent. But, if we must talk business, we do so with extreme caution."

After some time, my grandfather announced, "Soon, you will see something you will always remember."

As we continued to walk, we moved slightly away from the shore of the ocean to an area with many coconut trees. The large palm leaves blocked the light from the moon, creating an almost complete darkness in the space underneath them. We kept walking.

When we came to a hill of sand, we made our way to its top where we lay down to peer at the beach below.

My grandfather whispered, "Look over there. Look near the waves."

At first, I saw only a couple of rocks and the waves moving over them.

My grandfather directed me, "Pay attention to those rocks."

Suddenly, it hit me that the rocks were moving. Immediately, I knew that they were not rocks. They were turtles. There were three large turtles coming out of the ocean.

I looked at my grandfather.

He smiled and said, "The turtles will be at work real soon."

Very slowly and carefully the turtles crawled up the beach. Just as slowly and carefully, they began digging holes. In their holes, they laid eggs. They took great care to bury the eggs and refill the holes with sand. This was a long undertaking. The turtles' return to the ocean was also a spectacular process. It was a very smooth walk into the ocean. All you could see were the ripples of water from the waves going right over the humps of the turtles themselves. Gradually, they disappeared, almost as if someone had taken a great eraser and erased them right in front of us.

Once the turtles disappeared, I inquired, "How did you know that we would see this wonderful event?"

"Because I saw it when I was a child, and I have seen it many times. I walk by here almost every morning to work on the farm. Yesterday I determined that this was the morning that they'd emerge from the ocean."

I continued, asking, "How did you know in particular that they would be here today?" "The moon. The moon and its shape told me that the turtles were ready to lay their eggs."

As we walked back, we ran into two men carrying baskets on their backs. As they passed us, they greeted us, saying, "¡Buenos días!"

A few minutes later, my grandfather confessed, "Edgar, those two men also knew the turtles would be laying eggs this morning. They are going to gather the eggs to sell in the market today. If we go to the market, we can have them for breakfast."

In the market they would drop turtle eggs into hot water for just a minute and then pull them out. The eggs would look like soft ping-pong balls. Then they'd put a hole in the egg and drip in a little lemon juice and hot sauce. To eat it, you would squeeze it into your mouth and then toss away the squashed-down egg-shell. You could even make scrambled turtle eggs.

Before we reached home, my grandfather turned to me and said, "Edgar, you're meant for something big in life. I know that. And it's not becoming a farmer like me."

Edgar's grandfather showed him something magical that he had never noticed before. Is there anything in your world that you could observe more closely to discover something new and exciting?

Chapter 3

Papá's Healing Hands

My grandfather was correct. I didn't want to become a farmer. I had another dream. A big dream.

I was sitting on the sill of an open window in my family's small home. My eyes wandered the vast landscape in front of me while my mind dreamed.

It was amidst this daydreaming that my eyes lit on three faraway figures. Two of them were riding a horse, and one was leading it. What was striking—the first person sitting on the horse had two heads. I was seeing a two-headed man.

As they got closer, I started to doubt myself. "I must be wrong. How can it be—a two- headed man?"

When they got even closer, I could see that, in fact, the man did not have two heads. The second head was actually a large mass hanging from his neck. The mass was a huge ball of infection, the size of a melon. I could see that there was hair growing on this "second head" as well.

I realized the three were coming to see my father. Our home acted as the regional clinic, and Papá acted as the doctor-dentist. They were coming to get help for this man.

When they arrived, Papá emerged to stand in the doorway of our home. As was his custom, he was smoking a cigarette. He took a moment to look at the seemingly two-headed man—who appeared more dead than alive. After taking a long drag from his cigarette with an equally long exhale, Papá said to them, "Come on in."

The woman and the boy carefully helped the sick man to get off the horse. The man's name was Señor Timoteo. He was pale and weak. The large, hairy balloon of infection hung heavily from his neck. It took several minutes to get the man off the horse.

Papá asked Señor Timoteo, "How long have you been sick?"

The woman answered, "About three months."

"Has he been treated?" Papá asked.

She answered, "Several times the local healer put banana leaves soaked in kerosene on the infected area. Also, he had him drink a special mixture of armadillo and iguana oil while chanting some magic words."

"I see. Bring him inside."

Señor Timoteo was placed on a reclining wooden table my father designed to perform procedures on the head and neck. Papá carefully attempted to turn the man's head to the right and then left. However, the man's neck proved quite rigid, resisting my father's guidance. In this way, Papá assessed the ball of infection, determining how deep it went into the neck. Also, it helped him determine Señor Timoteo's level of pain, which was significant.

Papá told him, "I'm going to stick needles into your neck to ease the pain. Then I'm going to puncture the mass to release its pus. It will make you feel better fast."

He gave the man a drink of a special medicine to ease the pain.

The man did not flinch at all when my father cleaned the area with alcohol. With an aluminum bucket held against the man's neck, Papá made a small cut into the mass. A faucet of pus flowed from the ball of infection into the bucket.

I was sitting on a small wooden stool watching every move Papá made. I did not dare move. My father had a steady hand, always precise about what he was doing.

Gently Papá cleaned the man up, packed the deflated mass of a wound with iodine- soaked strips of sterilized bed sheets, and gave him antibiotics.

To Señor Timoteo he said, "Sir, you are amazing, you did wonderful. I can assure you that you will feel great by tomorrow, and you will be cured."

The man looked at Papá and for the first time showed some life. He gave a small smile.

Eight days later, Señor Timoteo returned. He looked, moved, and spoke like a different man. He could even ride the horse unassisted and dismount it with ease.

Papá removed the bandages.

Señor Timoteo was cured.

This was one of my father's many brilliant acts of healing that stands as legendary in my memory.

While my father always permitted me to observe his work with patients, when he worked with a child, I was able to do more than watch. I was allowed to assist. My job was to help them not to be afraid. To help them feel calm.

Once I saw my father take care of a 3.5-year-old boy. The boy, Carlitos, could hardly speak. His voice sounded strangled. He was very skinny. His mother said he didn't eat much. The problem was that Carlitos was "tongue-tied." This meant that his tongue had a malformation in it where a thick membrane connected too much of it to the bottom of his mouth. This limited his ability to move his tongue much, so much so it was difficult for him to eat or speak.

Carlitos was anxious. He did not smile. I wasn't sure he was going to pay attention to me, but surprisingly he did. He kept looking at me, following me closely with his eyes as my father was making preparations.

My father asked him, "Carlitos, do you like the ocean? Edgar loves the ocean and goes there all the time. Do you like the ocean?"

Carlitos nodded yes but said nothing. He started to cry a couple of times and made muffled sounds with his voice.

When his big eyes next searched me out, I spoke to him.

"*As visto una iguana?*" Have you seen an iguana?

He wrinkled his face like he was not really interested in talking about iguanas.

Then I said, "I was your age when I first saw one. I cried, and I was afraid to look at it and definitely did not want to touch it."

He smiled at my words.

My father told his mother, "Take this cloth and have him smell it slowly. He'll fall asleep for a few minutes, and I can work on his tongue."

Once the boy fell asleep, my father quickly opened his mouth. He placed moist cotton below the boy's tight tongue and gently pulled the tongue up. He pulled the tongue up and down, exposing the membrane.

All the while, my father was teaching me. "Edgar, see the membrane? It's too thick and needs to be cut, so he can move his tongue more."

The boy's mother looked as well. She was surprisingly calm as she held her son in her lap.

There was a quick "snip" sound. My father cut the unnecessary membrane.

A few seconds later, Carlitos awoke and started to cry but only for a moment.

Three weeks later, the boy returned. He was able to move his tongue normally now, and his speech sounded better. Also, he was eating more. Carlitos was on the road to good health.

After the boy's visit, my father said to me, "Remember, Edgar, it's usually the simple things that cure people."

It was from witnessing my father do such incredible acts of healing that the big dream for my life emerged. I dreamed of becoming a surgeon.

> **Edgar's father helped many people with his healing hands. Is there something special you can do to help others and make a difference in their lives?**

Chapter 4

Flying Iguanas

"Abuelito, do people eat iguanas?" I asked.

He replied, "Yes, and they're very tasty. They taste just like chicken."

He went on to explain, "Also, iguanas are really good for you. They are a lean meat. It's because they eat so well. They eat fruits, vegetables, and insects."

I added, "Green iguanas are thin and strong, and they can fly!"

"You think they can fly, but can they?" my grandfather asked.

I answered, "The first time I saw an iguana was at the market. A man had a pet iguana on his shoulders and I was scared of it. That man told me they could fly."

That happened when I was 3.5 years old. A man had come from the city to sell special fruits in the local market. In our village we were used to eating pineapples, papayas, mangos, and guavas, so the grapes and apples he was selling were special. The man's iguana sat on his shoulders like a fancy scarf. It had a long tail that moved fast. My parents asked me to touch the reptile, but I refused.

"I remember the man also said some iguanas have three eyes," I said.

My grandfather explained, "That's only somewhat true. On the top of their heads is a place where it looks like an eye used to be. Maybe the ancestors of today's iguanas had three eyes. What's amazing is that this area on the top of their head, though not an actual eye, can be used to detect changes in shadows and light. They can use it as a kind of clock or to sense danger. Today, when we go to see the iguanas, let's look out for this spot that looks like a third eye, and let's watch to see if they can actually fly."

My grandfather and I walked to a green patch of land located in a swampy area near where the rivers meet the ocean. The trees in the area had giant tree trunks with branches as big as the trees themselves. Iguanas lived there.

We walked through a watery marsh, dotted with water lilies. The water lilies had red, purple, and yellow flowers with fat, bright green floating leaves. Insects hummed around us.

In a lowered voice, my grandfather said, "Let's walk slowly." He did not mention to me that alligators also roamed the area, but I knew because I'd seen them in the past.

My grandfather moved with care. His hand sat ready on the handle of the machete hanging from his left hip. As we walked, periodically he chopped shrubs and low-hanging branches to open up walkways for us.

In a quiet voice, he explained, "See, Edgar, look, there are about fifty iguanas in that giant green tree"— he paused to point—"There are probably more, but they blend with their green and black coloring. Notice the black ones. They seem to prefer trees with dark trunks and leaves. This allows them to stay better hidden from predators, like snakes and large birds."

My grandfather leaned over and grabbed a small log. "I'm going to throw this log onto that tree branch. This will get the iguanas moving. Let's watch closely to see if they fly."

I looked up in the tree as he threw the log.

Soon I could see iguanas—each looked about five feet long including their tails—one after another, leaping from branch to branch. They seemed to use their long, strong tails in combination with the flexible end of the branch to propel themselves extra high into the air to land on a branch of a nearby tree. They essentially bounced on their tails, which gave the appearance of flying!

"Now I get it, Abuelito, they aren't flying. Instead, the end of the branch is their spring and with their tail, they bounce on the spring to the next branch!"

"Yes, Edgar. Do you notice how some are dropping into the water? They are good swimmers. They can even stay underwater—sometimes up to twenty minutes. Something else—when an iguana is getting chased by a predator, they swing their tail fast, back and forth, to distract the enemy. They can even dislodge their tail to distract a predator!"

"You mean they drop their tail from their own body?" "Yes, exactly! Aren't they incredible?"

"Yes, they are, but they look so rough and thorny—how can we eat them?"

"That's where your mother and I come in," he said. "After we catch one, I'll skin it to remove the rough exterior. I'll also have to pull out the guts because those are full of bad bacteria. It not only tastes bad but would be dangerous to eat. To be underwater for so long, they have to have great lungs. You'll see when I remove the lungs that they are different from the lungs of other creatures. Iguanas have a long transparent membrane for their lungs."

"How about Mamá? What will she do?"

"She will cook them, and they'll taste terrific. We'll have the meat with hot red sauce, tortillas, and rice. It's delicious. You'll see."

Indeed, he was right. That day we took home six iguanas and feasted for two days.

How did my grandfather hunt them?

First, he tried lassoing the iguanas as they emerged from the water, but they were too quick for him, scampering away before he could pull the lasso tight around their bodies. After that, he changed tactics, hitting them on the head with a hard thump from the dull end of his long machete.

Edgar had an exciting adventure with the iguanas. What is one amazing experience in nature that has inspired you? How can nature help you dream big?

Chapter 5

The Rope of Life

L et me tell you more about the swamp where my grandfather and I went to hunt the iguanas.

La Mira was framed by two rivers as well as the ocean. Because of this setup, something extraordinary occurred. There was a point where the fast-moving waters of the two rivers—going in one direction—met the strong waves of the ocean—going in another direction. At this point a violent collision happened. Water exploded high up into the air. It was as if water bombs were exploding over and over again. It was spectacular.

This shooting water ran off into the nearby land to form a swamp. The swamp was made up of both freshwater and saltwater. As a result, the fish and creatures in the swamp were unique.

My grandfather and I didn't just go to the swamp to hunt iguanas. We also went to catch the special fish, shrimp, and langostinos that lived there. In English langostino translates to "little lobster," but they aren't actually lobsters. A langostino is a kind of long crab. They can be found in salt water, fresh water, or in swamps, and they are slightly different depending on their environment. The ones we found in creeks tended to be skinnier with small claws. The ones from rivers were larger with larger claws. The ones from swamps were even larger with even larger claws. In the ocean, we caught real lobsters that had gigantic claws.

To hunt langostinos in the swamp required a special technique. First, it was critical that we avoid alligators. We kept away from alligator areas, but still we were on alert. My grandfather was so experienced, he could hear an alligator breathing and swallowing.

We searched for tiny rock crevices, about five inches wide. My grandfather would insert one of his rough hands inside the crevice. If a langostino was inside, it would latch itself to his hand. It would not let go, so it was my job to dislodge it as it clung to his fingers. The claws were long, so I would step on the creature's head, and—bingo!—it would let go immediately.

My grandfather never allowed me to insert my hands into the crevices. He'd say, "Let's keep your little hands in good condition because one day you'll need them to heal people." He believed in me and my big dream to be a surgeon.

One Saturday, my grandfather and I were going on a particularly special adventure. We planned to fish from a raft in the ocean. It wasn't just any raft, but one that my grandfather made himself. My grandfather built the raft out of palm tree logs tied together with ropes. It was the size of a rectangular table. It floated well and was easy to move around the water.

On this day we hoped to catch lobster, shrimp, crabs, and ocean bass. My mother wanted the seafood for a party. It was a party to celebrate the birthday of Edgar Schwartz, my godfather. I'll tell you more about him later.

My grandfather was aware that it is dangerous to be on the ocean in a small raft. He was prepared. He had a good paddle and plenty of rope. Rope was key to safety. He wrapped rope around my waist and my ankle, and attached me to the raft. He attached himself to the raft with a long rope tied to his ankle. The rope was long so that when he dove into the water, he could find the raft again.

Another way to be safe was to stay in calm water. My grandfather was careful that we stayed in a cove, not out in the open ocean. A cove is a small, protected bay. There are fewer waves, so the water is calmer. The water in the cove was about twenty feet deep, and the bottom of the cove was rocky. This was perfect because lobsters, crabs, and shrimp lived in the rocks.

After securing ourselves to the raft with the rope, we went out in the cove. Next, we threw two cages made of chicken wire into the water. They sat on the rocky bottom of the cove. We aimed to trap lobsters, crabs, and shrimp in the cages.

As we were dropping the cages in the water, we noticed two others approaching in a raft. It was a native man and his son. When they reached us, the man, in his native language, asked my grandfather if they could fish near us. My grandfather, who was half-native himself and who could speak some in the language, said yes.

The man and his son were short and muscular with round faces. The boy was my size, but he appeared to be a little older than me. The boy wasn't able to speak. Instead, he made humming sounds. His eyes appeared big and sleepy. His father's were the same.

Next, my grandfather told me, "Edgar, I am going down to check the traps. I will return shortly. If there's any issue, just ring the bell or pull on the rope that's attached to my ankle. Then I'll know to return quickly."

As he disappeared into the water, the rope uncoiled more and more, dropping into the ocean as he moved deeper. Normally it would take my grandfather about one to two minutes to go down and return. It was consistent every time, and I never worried.

The man also had a rope tied around his ankle and secured to the raft. He went into the water as well.

My grandfather returned and so did the man. We sat for a while as my grandfather prepared a spear. I admired the golden fish, shiny rocks, and swirling green sea plants in the water around us.

After a few hours, my grandfather wanted to check the traps again and spear a few more fish. He jumped into the water just as the man in the nearby raft was surfacing from the water. As the man started to climb up into the raft, suddenly he fell backwards down into the water. It was strange.

Immediately, the boy started to panic. He made loud sounds and repeatedly banged on a bucket with a rock. Even still, his father didn't emerge from the water.

Rapidly I pulled my grandfather's rope, signaling him to return. Again and again, I pulled the rope as hard as I could. I rang the bell attached to the rope. The boy was screaming, and I began to panic.

Finally, my grandfather surfaced from the water.

"Abuelo, something's happened. The man next to us fell into the water. I think he's drowning. He needs help."

Immediately, my grandfather swam to the other raft, got into it, and started pulling the rope. Very slowly, he pulled the rope to get the drowning man out of the water. It took great strength, and eventually, the man surfaced. Coughing and shaking, the man hung onto the side of the raft. My grandfather helped him get into the raft. His ankle was bleeding from the rope digging into his skin from when my grandfather was pulling on it.

The man coughed and coughed. Seawater came out of his mouth. He was trying to breathe. His son was quiet but still seemed scared. After the man could breathe normally again, he hugged his son.

Next, he explained what happened. On the man's first dive into the water, he went down too fast and hit his head on a rock. He felt dizzy, but he kept going. Later on, when he was getting out of the water, he fainted and fell back in. He was unconscious underwater for about two minutes. It was amazing that he survived.

My grandfather helped the man and boy bring in their underwater traps as well as bringing in ours. All of our cages were loaded with lobsters and crabs.

After we dragged our rafts out of the water and onto the shore, the man said something to my grandfather. Then he and his son walked away, hauling their day's catch in big sacks on their backs.

I asked, "What did he say?"

My grandfather said, "He said, 'I thank God and the moon for their guidance.'"

Edgar learned an important lesson about trust and survival. What is a challenge you have faced that taught you something valuable? How did it help you grow?

Chapter 6

My Godfather's Invitation

Before I was born, Edgar Schwartz came to La Mira from Germany. The German company he worked for mined for metals all over the world. After they tested samples of soil from our area, they understood it was rich with nickel and silver, so they sent Edgar Schwartz to set up and run a mine, Truchas Mine.

Edgar Schwartz was red-haired, tall, about six foot four, and muscular, with a well-trimmed beard. He had six identical outfits of khaki pants and khaki shirts and wore one each day. They were custom-made to fit him perfectly. They were so well pressed that even when he was working in the dusty, dirty mines, they showed no wrinkles. He had three different pairs of boots, all brown, thick, and military-looking, plus a brown belt.

He walked straight. His posture, stance, and walk resembled a soldier's.

He spoke excellent Spanish. He was kind to people and loved children. He was married but didn't have any children. His wife was a teacher in Germany. His parents were also teachers.

When he first came to La Mira, he did not have a place to stay. My family offered him a small segment of the house to live in. He ate his meals with my family. He and my father hit it off really well. My grandfather also appreciated him. Even after he found his own place to live, he came to our house many times a week to visit.

When I was born, there were two Edgars in our town, Edgar Schwartz and me. I was named after him, and he was named my padrino or godfather. He returned to Germany when I was 2.5 years old. Though many families hoped for this honor for their children, I was the only child to whom he was the padrino.

A few years later, Edgar Schwartz returned to La Mira to continue the mining work. As I was older, I was able to spend time with him, and we became close. I was probably the only child allowed into Truchas Mine.

Truchas Mine was made up of a single large tunnel that went about a mile deep into the mountain. It was big enough that a small train made up of carts on tracks could go into it. It was very dark inside. Anyone entering had to wear a hardhat and a headlight. There were little oxygen tanks inside the carts in case anything happened inside the mine that required additional oxygen.

My godfather once took me deep into the mine for a tour. It was cool inside. It had a metallic odor. I heard the sounds of the rails, like a small train choo-chooing deep inside the earth.

"Put your hand in here and feel these wonderful metals," my godfather said.

I placed my hand in several pockets of the mountain. I viewed the different types of metals with their variety of colors.

He explained that some of the precious metals were quite heavy and more valuable than the lighter ones. Some of the metals would be used in factories in Germany as well as all over the world to make tools that would then be used to make life a lot nicer and simpler for people.

"Edgar, it won't always be foreign countries, like mine, coming into Mexico to make use of its rich resources. Mexicans will come into their own and flourish. It will take some time, but it is going to happen," my godfather told me.

"I actually have inside information that my company will be required to leave in a few years when the president of Mexico decides to nationalize mining and other industries here. That means that Mexican companies will take over, and that's a good thing. That means Mexicans become the decision-makers over their own country's resources," he noted with a smile of approval.

Though I didn't exactly understand what he meant by Mexico "nationalizing" mining, I considered my padrino very intelligent, similar to my grandfather— although no one could really beat my grandfather.

When my godfather had dinner with us, right after dinner, he and I would have our own conversations. He would teach me math as well as problem-solving skills, to the point that I knew a lot more than the average kid my age. What he would do was choose a topic and then ask a lot of questions about it, with each question leading to another. He made it feel like a game, but it was a conversation to get me to think aloud and learn to think better, with his help, in order to solve a problem. It could be a math problem. It could be an engineering issue. It could be an exploration of underground sewer tunneling, something he had lots of experience in. At the end of the night, it felt as if my brain had a good workout.

My padrino helped my grandfather develop a drainage and water system on his farm with a large well to water his crops. But it wasn't just my family that was touched by my padrino's talents—it was our whole town. The people of La Mira revered him.

The local farmers tried to raise cattle for beef and milk, but they'd never been very successful. Fortunately, there was never a shortage of fish, so we ate a lot of fish. Even still, my godfather thought that he could make the beef industry work better. He invested his own money and conducted trainings with many of the ranchers to create a cattle-breeding area and other improved systems. The cattle ranchers often cited my godfather as a regalo de Dios, a gift from God, and commented how we were all very lucky to have him.

To reach the mine, Río Las Truchas, the smaller of the two rivers framing La Mira, had to be crossed. While there had been a small, temporary bridge that the miners had been using for years, it was not adequate for transporting the heavy metals on large trucks from the mines to the shore of the Pacific. There, every three months, the metals were loaded onto small boats and carried to a large ship that would then carry it to Germany.

So, my godfather, in conjunction with a team of dedicated Mexican engineers and workers, decided to construct a sturdy bridge across the Río Las Truchas.

I witnessed the construction of the bridge from the onset. It started with dynamite. One blast after another, they blitzed the edges of the mountain on each side of the river. These explosions caused huge amounts of rock and debris to break off the mountainsides and slide into the river.

My godfather explained to me, "With the dynamite, we're narrowing the river on each side. After we narrow the river, we're going to use metal and cement to create foundations for the bridge on each side. Then we'll build mighty pillars."

The sight of the dynamite blasting apart the mountain was wondrous. I thought to myself, "My goodness. All the things that I'm witnessing now—I wonder how many more spectacular things I will see in my lifetime."

I asked my godfather, "Padrino, have you ever blasted anything in Germany with dynamite?"

"Absolutely," he replied, "We used dynamite out there to do many things because in some areas we did not have resources to drill deep. We used dynamite for excavations."

He explained that they used dynamite to blast the rock out of large areas. Then they used that rock as a source of footings for buildings or for concrete to stabilize buildings and bridges.

I was impressed with my godfather's intelligence and life experience. I even pondered to myself, "If I can be as smart as my godfather and my grandfather, then I should have no problems in life."

During the months that they were building the bridge, I became closer with my godfather. I learned to appreciate everything that he would talk to me about. I felt like a sponge, retaining all he would say to me and the puzzles and problem solving he would challenge me with.

Finally, when the bridge was completed, I saw the mighty trucks, fully loaded with mineral-rich rocks, cross it.

My grandfather was with me, witnessing the trucks' first crossing of the bridge. He told me, "Come on over and get right close to the bridge. See how it doesn't move, even with the weight of the trucks. You could have twenty trucks crossing this bridge, and it will never move. It is solid. Edgar, you know why it's well built? It's because an expert team of Mexican engineers and workers along with your godfather came together to build it."

And the farmers and ranchers in our area were also grateful for the bridge because they used it to get their cattle and goods across the river.

I looked up at my grandfather as he smiled and swallowed a bite of mango. Wiping his beard, he added, "You, too, someday will become great like your godfather. He's a great engineer. You'll be a great surgeon. I'm certain."

It was around this time that my godfather met with my parents to deliver a special invitation.

He told them, "As you all know, in the next year or two, I'll return to Germany for good. My wife and I would love for Edgar to come live with us. I promise that Edgar will not only be loved, but he'll also get a great education. He can go on to medical school and become a top surgeon, just like he dreams."

Before discussing this amazing invitation, there's something I should explain about my family. I had seven siblings. Out of the eight of us, the four youngest and I lived with our parents in La Mira. That would be me, Lupe, Asunción, Reyna, and Manny.

Our three older siblings—Jorge, Surama, and Pedro—all left home when they were around ten years old. They left to go live with family members in far-away cities, where they had more opportunity for a good education and better future. It wasn't easy for my parents to allow their children to leave home so young, but they wanted us to have the greatest chance of living good, happy lives. They saw education as key to that.

I point this out to show that my padrino's invitation was realistic.

My parents gave their blessing that I could go to Germany with my padrino if that was what I wanted to do. It was my decision.

Edgar's godfather opened a door to new possibilities for him. Who in your life has encouraged you to see new opportunities? How can you be open to big possibilities for your own future?

Chapter 7

The Arrival

"Edgar, we have a surprise for you. Your half-brother Miguel will arrive today from the United States. He's looking forward to meeting all his little brothers and sisters," my mother told me.

In addition to my seven brothers and sisters, I had six older half-siblings from my father's two earlier marriages. (Sadly, each of his previous wives died from complications while giving birth.) My half-siblings were much older than me and my brothers and sisters, and they lived in faraway places, so we hadn't met many of them. Though I'd never met my half-brother Miguel— he was in his mid-thirties and lived in Phoenix, Arizona—I felt like I knew him. My parents regularly received letters from him, and it seemed everyone in La Mira knew him.

When Miguel arrived in La Mira, the whole town came out to meet him. Though he arrived in the morning, it took him several hours before he reached our house because so many people came out to greet him, shake his hand, and welcome him back. When he arrived at our home, he was surrounded by friends and village elders. Lupe, Asunción, Reyna, and baby Manny ran to him and warmly hugged him.

Instead of going forth with my brother and sisters, I stayed back and simply stared at him. I couldn't understand myself. Even at eight years old, I considered myself mature, brave, and ready to face anyone, but suddenly, it felt as if I'd been zapped by a strong magic. I stood frozen in awe. My brain knew I wanted to greet this fantastic older half-brother and hug him tightly—but my body felt stunned as if overcome by a spell. What was happening to me?

Miguel seemed like a movie star, and I felt too humble, too unworthy to be acknowledged by such a presence. I really didn't understand what had come over me.

I saw him embrace my grandfather warmly, and they talked for a moment. Next, he hugged my mother, and then my mother introduced him to my godfather.

I continued to hide—and watch him closely.

My younger sister, Reyna, encouraged me, "Edgar, go and say hi to our brother."

Noticing my strange behavior, my grandfather took my hand and brought me to Miguel, announcing, "Miguel, you must meet Edgar. There's nobody in this town like him. I think you'll find out what a special young man he is."

My grandfather went on to say that I was the hardest-working child in town. He also confided, "Edgar is the apple of my eye."

Miguel gave me a warm smile.

Again, I noticed the pounding of my heart—I still felt paralyzed by awe in the presence of this remarkable man.

My grandfather continued to stay by me.

My godfather, in his perfectly fitting khaki pants and khaki shirt, joined us.

Next, my father approached.

And so I found myself standing in a circle of fine men. I stared at my father, who had tears in his eyes, as he welcomed Miguel back home. My godfather radiated competence with his tall bearing and intelligent eyes. With a hand on my shoulder, my grandfather glowed with love, tranquility, and calm strength.

Miguel, moving nearer to me, said, "Mi hijo, my son, come here. Come close to me."

And just as strangely as that anxiety had come upon me—it disappeared. Total composure set in my body and spirit, and I moved close to Miguel.

Miguel put an arm around me, and I smiled with pride. I felt special. A signature move of my grandfather was putting his arm on the shoulder of anyone he really liked. This too was Miguel's gesture of affection and respect.

And so I stood with my grandfather's arm resting on one of my shoulders, and my older half-brother Miguel's arm resting on my other.

"Edgar, please take Miguel to the house and show him the room we've prepared for him," my mother told me.

Our house was made of adobe and had smooth dirt floors. The floors were cool, and I loved walking on them barefooted.

However, when showing Miguel our house, I found myself embarrassed about the dirt floor. I was afraid that my brother would be disappointed in what we had for his accommodations—a small mud-brick room with dirt floors.

Then I became afraid he'd ask about the bathroom. Our bathroom was an outhouse. I never even knew the possibility of a bathroom inside a home, so why was I embarrassed? I didn't know why, but I was.

Looking at me, Miguel asked, "Is this your room?"

"Yes, but now it's yours."

Miguel sat down on the bed, a square, wooden frame with a half-inch thick, circular *petate* for a mattress.

"This is quite comfortable," he noted.

I knew he was being polite.

"Where will you sleep?" Miguel asked.

"I'm staying with my sisters and my baby brother in the other room."

In this way, with his simple questions, warm manner, and kind observations, Miguel helped me to relax.

When I feel comfortable, I talk, and so I began talking. "Miguel, will you visit the ocean with me and Abuelito tomorrow? I'm going to miss a day of school, but don't worry. It'll be fine because I'm three lessons ahead right now. I'm usually ahead anyway, and César, my teacher who is really great, he won't mind if I take a day or two off, so I can be with you."

"Edgar, thank you for inviting me. Yes, I'd like to go, but maybe not tomorrow. Like you, I grew up here, but I haven't been back for many years, so I must visit the many people here who knew me as a little boy. I will be making some visits tomorrow. Does this sound good to you?"

"Yes, Miguel."

I noticed that his shoes were shiny. His pants were beautiful with belt loops, a zipper, pockets, and careful seams—not like the white sackcloth drawstring pants the kids and men of our village wore. And he was wearing socks, which I certainly was not used to seeing.

All of us kids wore *huaraches,* which are leather sandals. Their soles were constructed of actual pieces of old tires. Sometimes, when we walked on wet dirt, we almost left tire tracks. They were comfortable and solid. And we didn't wear socks with them, so seeing real shoes and socks was noticeable to me.

I asked Miguel more questions, "Do you speak English?"

"I speak some English, enough to do my work and get by. But I want to get better at it."

I confessed, "I would love to learn English."

Miguel assured me, "Don't worry—someday you will. Just wait your turn, and you will see. Something will happen."

"Miguel, why have you waited so long to visit?" I inquired.

"It takes time and money to make the trip here from the USA. I have a job, and people depend on me, so I don't want to take time away from work too often. And I have a car—"

"You have a car?" I interrupted.

"Yes, I have a car. And it needs new tires and certain repairs, but I didn't have enough money to spend on the car and on the visit, so I decided to make the visit. I would rather spend that money making this trip to meet you and visit the family."

At these affirming words I found the courage to say, "Miguel, let me tell you about our bathroom. First of all, it's outside like everybody's bathroom in town, but since my godfather designed it, it has a lot of features that make it special." I went on to show Miguel the bathroom and how it worked.

Eventually my mother found me and told me it was time to sleep.

Before leaving, I asked Miguel, "How long will you be staying?"

"Not too long. I want to spend as much time as I can with all of you, but I'll need to return to Phoenix to get back to work."

Although I'd known he was only visiting, not staying permanently, I felt disappointed when he confirmed it was just a short visit. Although I knew it was true, I simply refused to believe it.

Edgar's family welcomed Miguel home with love and excitement. If you could meet someone special who inspires you, who would it be? What would you ask them?

Chapter 8

The Cough

The next morning, Miguel invited me to accompany him on his visit to Chucho. Like my grandfather, Chucho was a farmer. He never wore anything other than the common dress of our village, the sackcloth shirt and drawstring pants. His skin was identical to my grandfather's—leathery and thick. He also wore a machete as my grandfather and about all the farmers did, strapped to his side at the hip.

Chucho had twin daughters but had lost his two sons, one from an infection and the other from falling off a wild horse. His wife died when giving birth to their twin daughters. Though she had eight children of her own, my mother cared for Chucho's twin girls, sharing with them the little milk that we had from our home, and this meant the world to Chucho. He always said that his girls were alive because of my mother, and anything that her children ever needed, he would be there to supply. Chucho was a man of his word, and he was like family.

When Miguel was a teenager, he'd had a dispute with our father and apparently had lived with Chucho for two months because of it. Chucho had been instrumental in bringing about a reconciliation between them.

When Miguel and I walked into the courtyard, Chucho met us, giving us hugs and inviting us into the kitchen where we smelled something absolutely delicious cooking on the fire. It was dried jerky mixed with eggs, simmered in a red hot sauce, and then served over white rice. It's a traditional breakfast called *aporreadillo*. Another way of eating it is with beans.

Miguel told us that he made the same breakfast in Phoenix. And while he could find all the ingredients and spices there, it just didn't taste as good. Somehow the food in our village tasted better.

Miguel and Chucho talked about everything, especially my father's health. It was obvious to everyone that Papá was very sick and his condition was only getting worse.

Unlike others that would say Papá had "just a little cough" or that he was "just sick but not that bad,"
Chucho refused to play down Papá's poor health. He
told Miguel the truth. He admitted that many times
our father's coughing scared him. Chucho argued that
our father was likely a lot sicker than he appeared and
that the only thing that could possibly help would be
if he quit smoking, but that our father refused to quit.

Chucho described how he'd witnessed Papá have
a horrifying coughing fit. It happened when Chucho
brought a man who'd fallen off a carriage and injured his
leg to get medical treatment with Papá. While Papá was
cleaning and closing the wound, he started coughing
severely. During the fit—which lasted for minutes—his
color changed from blue to gray to purple to ash.

"Miguel, the man with the hurt leg got so scared
of your father. I didn't know what to think myself—I
couldn't tell if it was the man or your father who most
needed medical help. Really, I was horrified. I didn't
know what to do, and that's why I wrote you, asking
you to return to see for yourself what's been going on,"
Chucho explained.

Papá's poor health wasn't news to me. Everyone in
the family had been witnessing his decline over the past
couple of years. So, rather than listen closely to them, I
allowed my mind to wander. I imagined how my life would
be if I lived with Miguel in the USA. I saw myself jump-
ing into a car with Miguel in the driver's seat. I imagined
rolling down the windows and the cool air hitting me as
I sat next to Miguel as he was driving. I imagined many

things—how it would feel to live there, to go to school there, to learn English. I wondered, "Can this dream come true, or is it just the imaginings of a kid?"

That evening, Miguel gave me an American dollar.

I looked at the dollar, declaring, "This is beautiful. It's so thick, not like Mexican bills. Mexican bills are really thin. They look cheap compared to this dollar."

My brother explained, "It's not that they're cheap. It's just that one American dollar is worth 12.5 pesos."

I asked, "So the thicker the bill, the more it's worth?"

"Yeah, I guess you could say that," he responded.

"A $5 bill or a $10 bill or a $50 bill must be really, really thick," I remarked.

"Sort of. They're certainly worth a lot of money. But the peso has value too."

I held the dollar, looking at it closely, the front and the back, through the sides, and up in the light.

"Who is the man on this bill?" I asked.

"It's George—in Spanish we say 'Jorge'—Washington, the first President of the United States. Every bill has the face of an American President on it," Miguel explained.

Before getting up, Miguel added, "Someday, Edgar, I'll talk to you more about what it takes to earn a dollar. I predict that in the future you are going to be earning lots of dollars."

A week into his visit with us, for the first time Miguel witnessed our father battling out a horrific coughing spell. He coughed and coughed and coughed. Meanwhile, his whole body turned blue. He seemed to be choking. His face was frightening. His eyes were sunken in, and his eye sockets got bigger and bigger and bigger. With all the shuddering, shaking, and thumping, it didn't seem possible that his frail body could continue to support him. He seemed to be coughing out his last bit of life. And it went on and on.

My youngest sister and baby brother were terrified and hid.

Miguel was very afraid and rushed to comfort Papá, to try to help in some way, but our father pushed him away. This back and forth went on repeatedly. It was a ghastly scene.

Though this was the worst coughing episode I'd yet witnessed, in a way I felt used to it.

Eventually, once Papá's coughing stopped, Miguel stepped outside and my mother followed. She went out to talk to him, discussing all the concerns she'd been holding back, her worries about the children, the family, their livelihood, and our father's likely fast-approaching death.

The following morning Miguel asked me, "Does Papá cough like that a lot?"

"Yes," I admitted. "I have gotten used to it, and I think all of us have as well."

I wish Miguel hadn't seen it because it changed him. He became worried. His spark was gone.

The next day at school, I heard other kids talking about Papá, saying terrible things: "Mr. Hernández is a walking skeleton," "My parents said he's forgetting things, that he's losing his mind," and "I heard he's going to die any day now."

Perhaps my dream of leaving with my brother to the United States was simply a way to escape the pain of our father's impending death and the pain of not knowing what would become of the rest of us after he died. No matter the reason, I was entranced by my older brother and the dream of living with him in the United States of America.

The following day I decided to talk to my grandfather. "Abuelito, I guess I've gotten used to Papá's coughing and his sickly appearance, so I stopped thinking about it. But now with Miguel and Mamá so worried, I'm wondering what you think."

"*Hijo*, I am so sorry you and your siblings and Miguel have to witness your father's coughing fits. That's a scary thing to see. But I must tell you—I fear this is only the start of your father's decline. He is going to get worse and worse. We must prepare for his death. That's why Miguel came here. You see, it's your mother and the children that he's most worried about. Your brother is selling a small coconut farm he owns, and most of that money is going to your mother, so she will have something in case something happens to your father."

"I didn't know. Miguel didn't tell me this," I replied.

"I figured he didn't—so I'm telling you. He's also donating some of that money to your school. He noticed how you all carry chairs from home to school and back each day, and he wants to change that. He's buying chairs for your school. Your brother is a fine man—a rarity. And I want you to be very strong when he leaves. It is necessary for him to return to the United States, so you must be brave and strong to help your brother have a good departure."

The dreaded day finally arrived.

My grandfather cooked two young goats. Also, there was corn, vegetables, watermelon, and guavas from his farm. It was a goodbye celebration.

But I didn't feel celebratory. My eyes were red and swollen from crying.

A large truck arrived. Two long benches lined each side of the truck's bed. This is where the passengers would sit, facing each other. The bed of the truck had a scaffolding over it onto which was strapped a yellow tarp to protect the passengers from the dust, heat, or rain. This was the truck that would take Miguel away.

From a distance I watched the goodbyes. The scene reminded me of Miguel's arrival, the way he'd been surrounded by people and the way I'd kept my distance. I saw Miguel converse with my godfather. Then they shook hands. Miguel hugged other friends and acquaintances. He then talked to my grandfather who wept as he hugged Miguel.

My grandfather then came out to where I was and placed his arm around me. I tried to resist more crying, but I could not hold back.

My brother knew he would have to deal with me sooner or later before departing. Amid the hugs and handshakes, he occasionally glanced in my direction, as if saying, "I haven't forgotten you. I'm coming."

He talked to my mother for a few minutes.

Finally, the moment came. I felt special, like I was onstage, frightened, yet full of emotions and tears. Then I suddenly stopped crying. My tears dried up as Miguel approached me. My grandfather left me to be alone with Miguel.

"Edgar, I loved returning to La Mira. I loved seeing my family and old friends again. The ocean and the food—it's been so wonderful. And you—you've been the highlight of my visit. I know a lot about you that you don't know that I know."

I quickly perked up, asking, "Really?"

My brother kneeled down slightly and put both his hands on my shoulders. He took his right hand to tap me on the chin, so I'd lift my head up and look him in the eyes. Then he told me, "Yes. And when I come back, it'll be because I'm coming to get you to bring you to America."

He gave me a hug. Then he walked back over and kissed my mother and father. After that, he stepped into the bed of the truck and sat at the end of the bench.

As the truck drove away, my brother waved at us, as if saying, "Goodbye for now, and I shall return some-day." Soon after, the truck kicked up a thick curtain of dust and Miguel faded from our sight.

Edgar witnessed his father's strength and struggles. How can you learn from the strength of the people around you to push forward in your own life?

Chapter 9

Sharing Dreams

César Fuentes, my teacher, came from an outstanding family of teachers. His grandfather, his father, his mother, and all his brothers and sisters were fine teachers. They taught in various areas in southern Mexico. They were talented individuals with one mission in mind—to make their students learn and become fruitful citizens of Mexico.

If all of Mexico had teachers like César and his family, no child would be illiterate. The Fuentes's had such a passion for teaching that their words alone seemed to enter the mind and straighten it out. They communicated a compassionate message to students that we conduct ourselves in the best manner, learn, and become educated so that we would grow into capable and responsible adults, and ultimately, we'd make our families and country proud.

My father had been key in getting César to come to our community to teach. At one time, my father was presidente of the town, which is sort of like being a mayor but not exactly. The presidente runs town meetings that address issues like children's immunizations and schooling. When the meetings addressed teacher recruitment, they were well attended because the community's main goal was educating its children. As presidente, my father did a lot of work to encourage César to live and teach in our town.

My father always told my siblings and me that our teachers were like our second parents and that we should respect them as such. My father was right— César was like a second parent to me.

He was young, energetic, dark-skinned, and good-looking. His teeth were so bright white he could have made a commercial for a toothpaste company. He wore white, short-sleeved shirts. The upper button of his shirt tended to be open, exposing the shiny skin of his chest. His biceps protruded below the rim of the short sleeves. He rode a bicycle.

César played the trumpet, violin, guitar, and accordion, and he could sing beautifully. At my grandfather's birthday party, César sang "Ave Maria," and it was quite moving.

He was a man of affection. He hugged all of his students, especially when comfort was needed. He did not like us to call him "Señor Fuentes." He wanted to be called "César."

César taught the second, third, and fourth grades, and seemed to know all the ingredients a child needed to get a good education. Because he felt that our class should be like a family, he had each of us take an oath at the beginning of the school year. We promised that if any of us fell behind in our studies, we would admit it to the class, and collectively the rest of us would work to help that student catch up.

César argued that while competition could be healthy, because there were many factors that affected a student's performance, we must be sympathetic and unify as a group so that all of us could come together and assist any of our classmates in need of extra help.

César had looked around when he was telling us this, saying, "It could be you . . . It could be one of you or you or you," pointing at each of us individually, "that falls behind and needs our help." We all agreed that we would work together and help each other.

The next day at school, the day after Miguel departed, César announced, "Today, students, we're going to talk about dreams. What do you dream for yourself in life? What are your dreams for happiness and success? Young minds have dreams very different from those of adults. Adult dreams often get mixed up with responsibilities and society's expectations. Young people's dreams tend to be clear, positive, and creative. Dreams are planning for the future. After all, the more aware you are of your dreams—the more you can describe them, see them, and know them—the more likely you can make your dreams come true!"

Turning to one of the students, César said, "Juanita, do you have a special dream in life?"

"Oh, yes, sir," Juanita responded.

"Will you stand at the front of the classroom and tell us about your dream?"

Once she situated herself in front of us, Juanita said, "I have a lot of life dreams, but my main dream is that I want to be a coconut farmer."

"Please tell us more," César encouraged her.

"It's because I know coconuts really well," she answered. "They have great-tasting juice and meat within. My father and I extract oil from their meat, and we sell that oil in the market. I see myself working with coconuts in the future."

"So you want to sell coconut water, coconut meat, and coconut oil?" he asked.

"Yes. And I could imagine making body lotion from coconuts as well."

We were impressed with her confident vision.

"Thank you, Juanita." To the rest of us, César said, "Did you all hear Juanita's clear, strong response?

Notice how her dream is based on her interests, not on what's popular. Who would like to speak next? How about you, Sonia, what are your dreams?"

Sonia was very shy, so César gently encouraged her to stand at the front of the class and speak, saying, "Sonia, most of your classmates are frightened to speak as well. You need not worry, just tell us about your dreams."

Looking down, she replied, "Yes, César," and she quietly walked to the front of the classroom.

Sonia was a tiny girl with big eyes and a pony-tail. Her mother was a seamstress and made colorful dresses worn by most of the women in the village.

She began, "I have dreams, but I can't put them together. It's like they are in pieces, hiding from me."

"Anything you remember?" César asked.

"Well, my parents only have me. My sister and brother passed on."

"If you don't want to talk right now, we can wait for another day. It's okay with us, isn't that right, boys and girls?"

We all said yes.

With Sonia still standing there, César told us, "Did you know that when I was young, I dreamed of becoming a teacher, just like my grandfather, my father, and my mother? I knew that when I was your age. Dreams have a way of leading you to a path that only you and your dreams know. They can be personal, so if any of you don't want to talk about them, it's okay. It's just that I happen to have a class of dreamers—Edgar there wants to be a surgeon, Leonardo wants to be a lawyer, and Donato an engineer. Whatever people want, they can have. I want to get your imaginations going. I want each of you to live successful lives where you are happy and you make the world better. I, for one, still dream, I dream of making life-long learners out of everyone here."

"It's okay, César," Sonia said. "I'd like to share my dream. You see, I want to be a nun, una monja, just like my aunt who lives in the city. I remember talking to her about it. It's my life dream—to be a nun."

"Sonia, thank you for sharing your dream. So, children, what do you have to say to Sonia?"

He knew what our response would be—a loud applause as if we'd just won a prize.

My classmate Pablo Herrera was a memorable dreamer. He was eight years old. Strong, husky, with a smile painted on his face. He looked at life as precious. He was mild mannered and polite. He never complained. Pablo came from a very poor family. He lived with his father and sister. Pablo was mostly deaf, hearing only slight noises. His way of "hearing" was through lip-reading. When he spoke, it was in a whisper. Not only was he challenged by deafness, he also had a shorter than usual right leg. Also his right leg was thinner than the left one, and it was wobbly. His sandal often had to be tied up high on his ankle.

Though he was deaf, Pablo loved playing music. He could play the guitar, violin, and drums, but he could not hear what he was playing. His songs were brief, and at times he would hum and close his eyes.

Pablo's sister also had a physical challenge. She was blind. She sang and played the guitar. Even with their physical challenges, the two of them made music.

So, what was Pablo's dream? What was his main wish and hope in life?

When Pablo spoke to the class, this is what he said: "Yes, I have a dream. It's one I have every day and night. My dream is that someday my sister will be able to see. I pray and dream that someday she can see."

What a humble and beautiful dream. The class clapped and cheered for Pablo.

There wasn't enough time for all of us to speak that day in class. Along with some fellow classmates, I would share my dream the following day.

After school César asked to speak with me. He told me, "You know that I've known your brother Miguel for many years. I met with him before he left, and he told me that he wished he could take you back to the USA with him, but he thinks the family would fall apart without you here."

I was taken aback.

César paused for a moment and then continued, "I told him that I totally agreed."

"How is it both of you think of me in this way?" I asked.

"Edgar, with your father's health problems, your family needs someone to brighten their lives. I think they would miss your constant talking, your questions, your curiosity—something you don't just share with your family but with everyone. Everybody in town adores you."

That night, instead of relaxing and dropping into sleep, my mind churned with questions and possibilities. "Even though I didn't leave with him this time, what about in a year or two—could I move to the USA with Miguel? What will happen to my mother and me and my siblings when Papá dies? My godfather has given me an open invitation to go to Germany with him. Do I want to go to Germany? Would I rather move to Germany or the USA? Maybe I should stay here. It would be so difficult to leave my grandfather, and my family really needs me."

My true feeling, deep in my mind and heart, was that I wanted to go to the USA with Miguel. I would study and become a surgeon. Eventually all my family would go to the United States too. That was my big dream.

The next day at school, that's the dream I shared with my classmates.

> **Miguel encouraged Edgar to dream about his future. If you could do anything in the world when you grow up, what would it be? How can you take the first step toward that dream today?**

Chapter 10

A Promise Kept

I
t was 1959. In the year and a half since Miguel visited, Papá's violent and bloody coughing episodes continued more and more frequently. His activity level dramatically decreased. He moved less and less. Eventually he did not go outside the house at all. His appetite was poor, and he lost about seventy pounds. My father's decline was striking and sad to see.

Eventually, one morning I heard my mother crying. When I saw her, I immediately knew what had happened.

"Get your grandfather, and call your godfather as soon as possible," she directed me.

My grandfather and my godfather immediately began making funeral arrangements.

The news spread, and family, friends, and neighbors came to our home to offer their condolences. César was one of the first to come over. He tried to console my mother. Then he left to send a telegram to Miguel.

Later César returned to tell us that he'd received news that Miguel was in the hospital with a serious infection and was not able to travel. Miguel's doctor would not allow him to leave the hospital for a week, at least, but as soon as he could, Miguel would be coming.

We proceeded with the burial because it could not wait.

I was surprised that I did not cry. When I asked myself why, I realized that I knew how greatly my father had been suffering and because of that, his dying seemed a kind of mercy, a relief from his pain.

At the burial I looked at my mother who was weeping, and I felt such intense love for her. With my gaze I tried to tell her that I loved her. She smiled back at me as if she'd heard my whisper. Similar to me, I think she understood that my father's death was for the best because it meant his suffering had ended.

The next day my grandfather and I visited the ocean together, and on this visit I truly felt in my heart, mind, and spirit that I would be leaving soon. I would miss the wind, the breeze, the moon, and the wonderful walks and times I'd spent with my amazing grandfather. All of this I would profoundly miss—and I could already feel the sadness of saying goodbye.

While walking the shoreline together, my grandfather told me, "Your dear brother is coming soon, and you'll be going back to the United States with him."

"How do you know that?" I asked in response.

"I know it, and I know you believe it to be the truth too."

He added, "This will be the beginning of a new life—of challenges and achievement—for you, *hijo*."

When Miguel arrived, we all were there to greet him.

Much to my surprise, I had no anxiety. I felt total tranquility at Miguel's arrival.

Miguel was weeping as he walked to us. "I am sorry I wasn't here. I am so sorry," he uttered. He explained that he'd had an infection on his neck that had gone up into his scalp and required two surgeries. We could see the two large cuts on his neck and scalp and the bandages in those areas.

I hugged him. I cried. My grandfather also cried.

Miguel asked that my grandfather and I accompany him to the cemetery.

At the cemetery, the air felt cool and the wind was strong, pushing through the large trees that surrounded the graves. The trees' long, finger-like branches moved, as if motioning us to come closer.

Dry, veiny leaves, the size of men's hands, swirled in the air and fell around us with a crackle. The scene felt eerie and alive with the presence of the dead.

Miguel approached the fresh grave inscribed with my father's name and fell to his knees.

"Papá," Miguel began, "I beg for your forgiveness because I wasn't here for you at your funeral. Please forgive me. Papá, I will miss you greatly, and although I have been away for many years, you were always on my mind."

At this point my grandfather and I began to walk away to give Miguel some private time at the graveside, but he turned to us, saying, "Don't leave. Stay here by my side."

He told my father, again as if conversing with him, "I will be taking Edgar with me back to the United States, and I want your blessing."

At these words the wind seemed to slow and the trees ceased their movement. A feeling of calm descended.

I looked at my grandfather, smiled, and hugged him. Then I went to my brother and hugged him. I cried for a while. I hugged him again, and I continued to cry.

My grandfather placed his right arm around my shoulder as a sign that he approved.

We were scheduled to leave in five days.

I needed to think about how I was going to tell my godfather that I would not be going to Germany with him. This was probably the most difficult thing that I needed to do.

The following day, after breakfast, I set off to the mines to visit him.

When I got there, I put on the hardhat and protective gear, and stepped into a cart with my godfather. We proceeded into the mineshaft.

"It's good to see Miguel again if only for a few days," my godfather stated, as if supplying me with an opening because he must have known why I wanted to speak to him.

"Padrino, I've decided that I'm not going to Germany with you. I am going to leave with Miguel back to the United States," I told him.

He stopped the cart, and with tears in his voice said, "Edgar, I am very happy for you. You belong with your older brother. And at the same time, I am sad for myself. You will be in the United States, and I'll be in Germany, and I will probably never see you again. You have a great future ahead of you, Edgar. I love you, and I'll always think of you."

The last few days went by quickly. My mother seemed happy, like a huge load had been taken from her shoulders. She told me to write her letters, be obedient, be smart, be a good student, and remember always that my teachers in the United States were the same as in Mexico and I should consider them like second parents.

She bought me a small toothbrush and a comb, advising, "Take a shower every morning. Brush your teeth and comb your hair. It is very important you take care of your teeth, so you can eat well and grow well. Your hair must always be in place, neatly combed. Your hands and nails must be clean and cut. You should act just the same as when both your teacher and I are with you."

I looked at my mom and felt like crying, but I didn't know if I had any tears left.

The day before my departure, my grandfather took me to a shop, explaining, "*Hijo,* we're going to get you a new, crispy white sackcloth shirt. It's important that you look good for your trip. Your *huaraches* are still in good condition. I think they'll last you a bit longer. Once you are in the United States, you probably won't be wearing them anymore. I imagine you'll start wearing shoes."

We enjoyed our last coconut popsicles together, which were a favorite of my grandfather's.

"Never forget all these wonderful things that you and your *abuelito* enjoyed together, like these wonderful coconut popsicles. Always remember me and the good times we had together," my grandfather told me.

The following day, we were set to go.

I embraced my mother. She was smiling, not crying. My grandfather hugged me and said, "You know what to do."

I replied, "I know."

I hugged and kissed my sisters and brother.

Once again, as the truck drove away, it kicked up a thick curtain of dust so that our family soon faded from our sight.

Edgar faced big changes in his life. What big changes have happened in your life? How did you choose to face those changes?

Chapter 11

Heading North

A man sitting on the bench seat opposite us asked, "*¿A dónde van?*" Where are you going? Miguel replied, "We're traveling north for the next few days."

"You must be going to the border—*la frontera.*"

"*Si, eso es correcto,*" Miguel confirmed.

The man smiled, saying, "You two are extremely lucky."

Miguel then turned to me to ask, "Can I see your birth certificate?"

I opened my small bag, and there was my birth certificate, an official letter from my mother in an envelope, and other important documents.

Miguel explained, "These are very important documents because we need them to get your visa. It's going to be several days to the border. We'll do some paperwork there and wait a few days to get your visa. After that, we will cross and be home."

"Miguel, what's a visa?" I questioned.

"It's a special document issued by a country with your name on it that says you are in the country legally," he explained.

Miguel then removed a card from his wallet and showed it to me, explaining, "There are different kinds of visas. This is mine. It's called a green card." It was a thin card that sat in a protective clear plastic sleeve. It had zigzag lines running across it horizontally.

"Notice that it states that I'm a legal resident of the United States. That means I can live and work there."

Miguel noted, "Edgar, it might be a bit tricky to get your visa quickly, but I know it can be done. I managed to get mine, and I helped your sister Olivia and your brother Pedro get theirs."

Miguel continued, "I bought a house in Phoenix. I'm still working on it, and I have a lot more to do. But soon, it will be a home that we can be comfortable living in."

I smiled and got close to him.

He told me, "In Phoenix, I work as a silversmith making Navajo jewelry."

I asked, "What does that mean—'Navajo'?"

He explained that the Navajo were a tribe of native people in the United States, similar to the Purépecha and the Tarascans in Michoacán.

Miguel explained that in 1951 when he was first trying to get his papers together to immigrate to the United States, he was in Nogales, the border town where he and I were going. Because getting the proper documentation and paying for it was difficult, he ended up finding work in Nogales at a jewelry store.

An American named Bernard Lambert got to know him because he was interested in some of the jewelry pieces Miguel had made. Mr. Lambert was so impressed with Miguel's work that he offered him a job in the United States. My brother explained to Mr. Lambert that he didn't yet have immigration papers or the money to pay for the process but was working on it.

Over a few weeks my brother got to know "Doc" Lambert and his wife, Margaret. They came to really like each other, so much so that the Lamberts sponsored Miguel's entry into the USA and helped him attain the needed paperwork.

The Lamberts owned a store that sold Navajo jewelry in Phoenix. After sponsoring Miguel with the immigration requirements, they promised him and the US government that he'd have a job waiting for him in Phoenix. This made his immigration possible.

When he arrived in Phoenix, he lived in a small apartment above the jewelry workshop. "We'll be living there for a while until I finish renovating the house."

He explained that the Lamberts' business was actually the biggest Indian jewelry wholesale business in Phoenix and had over forty employees, all Navajo Indians with the exception of Miguel.

"As a matter of fact," Miguel confided, "I speak better Navajo than English. Because I spend forty or more hours a week with 39 Navajo men, I'm fluent in the Navajo language."

Pausing to look out of the back of the truck, Miguel then explained, "It will take us several hours to get to Uruapan today. You'll be amazed by Uruapan. It's a city with electricity. It's got street lights, and there's even lights that control the traffic. You'll see the lights turn green, red, and yellow. Green means that cars can go. When it's red, cars must stop. The yellow means cars just take it easy—they can move forward or stop, depending on what makes the most sense."

Honestly, I didn't know what he was talking about.

He continued, "Soon, Edgar, you will see a television and a telephone."

As a nine-year-old child from a village in Mexico in the year 1959, I had some experience with electricity. It came from generators and was used rarely, only at special events a few times a year. However, I'd never seen street lights or stop lights. I'd never heard of a television or a telephone.

"What are those?" I asked, puzzled.

My brother explained, "A television is a kind of box with lights in it. It's kind of like a radio, but you actually see people as well as hear them. And a telephone is a machine for talking to someone like they are near you, yet they are very far away."

From the way he described these machines they sounded magical. I was both curious as well as a bit afraid.

Upon arriving in Uruapan, I couldn't contain myself. I had never seen such a beautiful place. There were green trees throughout. I noticed stalls loaded with the loveliest-smelling fruits, fruits that I wasn't used to seeing—pears, apples, and peaches. The air temperature was noticeably cool, not steamy and hot like La Mira.

Miguel advised, "Let's get to the hotel and take care of accommodations. We're going to have another long ride tomorrow to another city called Morelia. If you think this city is beautiful, wait till you see Morelia."

At the hotel, to the right of the desk counter, stood a large box with a curved piece of glass making up one of its sides. Music and conversation and people in shades of gray appeared in the glass. It was a television. I was pleased to discover that it wasn't scary at all. In fact, I found it wonderful.

Just standing inside the hotel we could hear layers of honking from cars on the street outside. While the hotel staff prepared our room, Miguel and I walked outside, and there before us—a multitude of boxy, metallic, wheeled rats racing around a maze. It was approaching dark, so headlights started turning on in the cars. It was marvelous to see and hear the multitude of squawking cars with brilliantly lit orbs beaming from their fronts.

Our room was on the highest floor of the hotel, and looking out the windows from up there, I felt like I was miles up in the air. In reality, the hotel was only three to four levels high, but to me, the height was staggering. Out the windows I could see the many cars with their glorious beams of light shining before them. Also, I saw shimmering strokes of light shining from the windows of other buildings. A city with electricity at night—I'd never seen anything like it before in my life.

Later, as we were finishing dinner downstairs, Miguel asked, "Do you see that object on top of the counter? That's a telephone. You can pick that telephone up and call any place in Mexico. As a matter of fact, you can probably talk to anyone in the world."

"Do you think we could take a closer look at it after dinner?"

After dinner, we approached the device. Miguel explained, "You pick the telephone up here and dial the numbers here. Everybody has a different number. When you get to Phoenix, you'll have a number."

"Really? I will have my own number?" I asked excitedly.

"Well, not exactly your own number, but we hope that we'll have a telephone in our house once the house is ready—and that telephone will have a number. We'll also get a television."

That was unbelievable—our own telephone and our own television too!

The next day, rather than a truck, we rode in a real bus. The road started ascending and the bus climbed higher and higher. At the summit I could see Morelia, a city even more spectacular than Uruapan. The whole scene was sensational. The road going into Morelia was lined by stately trees that I had never seen before—tall, thick in diameter, with dark green tassels.

I asked my brother, "What type of trees are those? I have never seen them before."

"It happens that in Morelia it gets really cold, and it even snows. In the types of places where it snows, you find pine trees. You're not going to see them in Phoenix. But up north past Phoenix, there's snow, and you'll be able to see the same kind of tree."

Pine trees surrounded the Morelia bus station too. After getting off the bus I walked to one of the trees and pulled a small branch down to my face. I breathed in the unique scent of pine—crisp, woody, sappy, tingly effervescence—a scent I had never before experienced.

When I returned to Miguel, I promptly asked, "So there's trees like this to the north of Phoenix? How big is Phoenix? Is it bigger than Morelia?"

"Yes, Edgar, it's bigger than Morelia. Phoenix's buildings are bigger, and there are more of them. The difference is that Phoenix is flat, it's spread out, and it is terribly hot during the summer, something that you'll adapt to with time."

He went on, "To deal with the heat, we have swimming pools."

That was something else I had never heard of before, so he explained to me what a swimming pool was. Again, it sounded unreal, dreamlike, this United States of America.

The next day we took a bus to Guadalajara and from there we took a train. While I had seen pictures of trains, I had never seen one in real life or ridden in one.

My brother explained that as we slept, the train would take us way up north and we'd wake near the border.

All night, I could not sleep due to my excitement about the train ride and my anticipation about our final destination. I knew we were getting closer and closer.

I was not worried when my brother told me he would place me in a school in Phoenix soon after we arrived. He said I would have to learn English really quickly so I could do my schooling and not fall behind. This challenge did not bother me. In fact, I was looking forward to it. I remembered that my godfather was born in Germany and spoke German, yet he became fluent in Spanish.

I tossed and turned, thinking of what my teacher would look like, what type of friends I would meet, and how it would be to speak English fluently. I imagined myself riding a bicycle, roller-skating, and playing baseball, things I had wanted to try but could not do because we didn't have these options in La Mira.

I think I only slept one hour, and I woke happy and ready to go.

I'd thought the train was going to take us directly to Nogales, the border town, but that was not the case. The train took us to Hermosillo, a charming town that was filled with red flowers. Every place that I looked, I saw flowers in bloom. I think that that was the reason they named it Hermosillo because hermosa means "beautiful," and in this town there were lovely flowers along the streets, along the sidewalks, and in many homes.

From Hermosillo, we had to take one more bus to reach Nogales. After that, we would finally cross the border.

On the bus to Nogales, Miguel explained that he had made arrangements to have a few people help us with the process of immigration. This concept of immigration was a curiosity to me. I knew we needed documents and that we had documents, but I did not understand the specifics. In our travels I'd heard bits and pieces about difficulties communicating with the American immigration officers and how all the regulations could be confusing. I wondered how long it would take us to get the documents I didn't yet have.

Finally, we arrived in the busy, fast, and noisy city called Nogales.

Miguel explained, "Americans come to Nogales and buy home-building goods like timber, tiles, roofing materials, and even home decorations. Then they resell them to other people in the United States who use them to construct large, fancy homes called 'mansions.' Nogales is a city where a lot of people do a lot of business. It's a very active city as you will soon see."

And Miguel was correct. I would soon come to know very well the hustle and bustle of Nogales.

Edgar took a big step toward a new life by traveling north. If you had the chance to go on a great journey, where would you go and why? What would you hope to learn?

Chapter 12

Lightning Bolt

The next morning, we met with Aurelio, a lawyer who would help us with the immigration process.

When Aurelio entered the room, he was so tall that he had to hunch down to fit under the door. His face was skinny and long. He had droopy eyes, droopy skin, and very long arms. His wrists stuck out three inches beyond the end of his shirtsleeves.

When Aurelio spoke, he spoke very softly. In trying to hear him, I thought I might have a problem with my ears. My brother later confided that he had to pay very careful attention to what Aurelio said because of how quietly he spoke.

Miguel explained that he hoped Aurelio could help us get the documents for my visa.

"Miguel, I'm happy to help you, but you should know that the process of immigration is more complex and it takes longer than it used to. It is not as straightforward as it was when you did it for yourself and Olivia and Pedro."

Aurelio then wrote a list of the documents he expected we would need:

One—a letter from Mr. Lambert, regarding Miguel's work

Two—proof of Miguel's housing: a rental agreement or documentation of home ownership

Three—a letter regarding Miguel's financial status and potential debt

Four—a police record

Five—if Miguel owned an automobile, proof of ownership

Six—letters of reference from three coworkers

Seven—a character reference from a church or a friend outside his work

Aurelio advised Miguel to get started immediately. He directed us to another room that had five telephones in different crevices on the wall.

Naturally, I was delighted to see so many of these futuristic talking machines. Plus, I'd get to watch Miguel use one!

From his phone calls, we learned that it would take about ten days for all of the letters and documents to get to us in Nogales.

After ten days, we had every document and met with Aurelio again. Aurelio scanned all the documents for a final review. He looked at every piece of paper, page by page, line by line. Finally, he looked up at my brother and announced, "You did a great job. These letters speak very highly of you. I am impressed. You are ready to go to the Consulate. You have all the needed documents, so I feel confident about your success."

Miguel and I walked to the Consulate. Once there, we took a number and found seats. The room was almost full. There were young people, single people, married people without children, couples with children, and elderly people. There was a very old couple, and the man resembled my grandfather with his weathered skin, long, white beard, and white sackcloth clothing.

I made conversation with people. I talked to a teacher who said it had taken him three months to gather all the documents needed to start his application. Other people had little understanding about the documentation. Some were given guidance by friends or strangers they'd met in the streets of Nogales. I felt that some of them were completely lost.

I concluded one thing—communication was a real problem for them. Many didn't know how to read or write themselves. Many didn't know how to articulate the kinds of questions to ask to determine the documents they would need. I explained how they could find Aurelio and that Aurelio might be able to guide them.

Finally, our number was called.

Miguel and I walked down a hallway and entered a small room. A pretty lady with golden hair entered. She asked for all the documents. She spoke perfect Spanish. She arranged all the documents and began examining each one.

She told my brother, "You have very nice letters, and you should be proud of all the things your friends and your employer said about you."

Then she asked about our father and his death. She said, "I'm sorry about your loss."

Next, she asked about a death certificate.

My brother pointed out, "I didn't think a certificate of our father's death would be necessary because we have an official letter from Edgar's mother granting me power of attorney over Edgar. This grants me total responsibility for him."

"I'm sorry, but we have to have a copy of the official death certificate. This certificate has to be signed by the official in the city of Uruapan, Mexico. Without it, it suggests that Edgar's father may be alive and not in support of that letter from Edgar's mother."

"How long do you think it takes to get a death certificate filed, so we can get a copy to you?" my brother inquired.

"It could take a few months to a year. It's a long process," she replied.

It felt like a lightning bolt of bad news had just struck us.

Later, at Aurelio's office, he expressed surprise and aggravation. He agreed that it could take months and as long as a year to get the certificate on record.

Aurelio told us, "Please listen carefully. Let's entertain something that could work on a temporary basis, but you both will have to be strong and listen to my idea."

Miguel and I leaned in even closer to hear his proposal.

"I am in the business of aiding people to enter the United States legally. My oath forbids me to do the contrary. However, a temporary illegal entry may buy us some time while we wait for the document."

Startled, my brother asked, "Are you suggesting that Edgar cross illegally?"

With a shameful look on his face, Aurelio responded softly, "Unfortunately . . . yes."

> **Edgar faced a dangerous moment but kept moving forward. Have you ever faced a moment when you had to be brave? How did it shape you?**

Chapter 13

The Plan

A fter exiting the office, Miguel told me he needed
to make some phone calls.

While I was waiting for my brother, worried
thoughts churned in my mind. I imagined all those
people waiting in that big room to see the immigration officers. Like me, they had filled their reservoir of
hopes and dreams with one grand plan—going to the
USA—but some couldn't read or write. They had very

little money. The process was a huge beast that could never be satisfied. And once they went in for the interview, that beast would tear a hole in them and begin devouring their dreams.

From there, my mind started spinning. "Are my mother, my grandfather, and the rest of the family okay? Are my sisters and my brother well? Do they have enough money to eat? Do they have enough to live on?"

Then I started thinking that perhaps it was a mistake for me to be here. Suddenly it felt selfish for me to try to go to the United States. "I should be thinking more about the rest of the family, rather than thinking only about myself."

I was feeling worse and worse by the minute. I found myself repeating, "It's a mistake for me to be here. I know it's a mistake. My dream to go to the United States is selfish."

I cried. I called out softly on several occasions, "Abuelito, Abuelito, what can I do? Please forgive me."

When Miguel found me again, I was crying. "Miguel, I'm sorry. It was a mistake for me to leave the family. I'm creating so many problems. I know you need to get back to Phoenix and work, and now you can't do it."

"Do not worry, hijo. I spent a while talking with Doc and Margaret Lambert about our situation and the additional document. I told them everything. Now I want to tell you what we decided. Before I tell you, know that you're going to have to be strong. Do you think you can do that for me?"

"Yes. I will be strong, no matter what."

"I'm going to take you across to the United States illegally. I don't want to do it this way, but as Aurelio said, it's the only way forward right now. If I wait here with you for a year, I'd lose my job, my car, and my house. With those things lost, the Consulate would never grant you a visa. If I go to Phoenix and send you back to La Mira, I worry that I'd never have the opportunity to go and get you again. So, though the plan is wrong, it is still the right decision. And I promise we will return and get you a proper visa."

"Miguel, I'm not scared. I'll do whatever you want me to do," I replied.

"Edgar, this is only a temporary fix. I promise."

"Miguel, I understand."

"This is how it's going to work. At the border crossing there's an entry-exit gate for people crossing by foot. There is an American officer who works that gate, and you will ask him if you can walk through to the US side—and he's going to allow you."

I wasn't sure what he meant by this. Why would an American officer whose very job was to protect the gate from illegal crossings allow me to walk through it?

Miguel continued to explain, "You're going to have to work hard over the next three weeks to make it happen. It's not going to be easy, but after the hard work, the crossing itself will be simple."

The following day, Miguel and I went to look at the entry-exit gate. Miguel pointed out, "You see how many people are walking through? And the restaurant across the street from it is busy. I think the officer working the gate right now seems like a nice guy—much friendlier than other officers. And he loves to eat. I've noticed that he's always eating."

At that moment, the officer was eating tacos and leaning on a bench. A few people approached and showed him some type of identification, and he waved them through. All the while he just kept on eating and smiling. There was a good nature about the man.

"I think that I'm going to like him, and I think he's going to like me real soon because he likes to eat what I like to eat—bean tacos," I said.

My brother asked, "How do you know that's what he's eating?"

"Because I've been eating bean tacos all my life. I'm an expert at identifying them."

The plan was that over the next three weeks, I'd take a crash course in English and I'd use that English to make friends with the border officer. The idea was not that I would try to become fluent in English—that couldn't happen in three weeks. Instead, I'd learn some basic phrases to befriend the officer. Then if the officer felt comfortable with me as a so-called friendly kid, maybe he would allow me to go through the gate to run a "quick errand" across the border.

It took me a day to learn a few English phrases and sentences—Excellent. Good morning. Hi, how are you? My name is Edgar. What's your name? It's nice to meet you. My favorite food is bean tacos. Have a good day. Take care. Goodbye.

As I walked around Nogales, I found myself repeating English phrases. Then I made sentences. I mixed words and tried to play around with them. I sang the phrases—anything to make them stick. I was trying hard to have all of the English words stay with me so that I could communicate with the border officer as soon as possible.

In the afternoons across the street from the entry-exit gate, I started playing soccer with a group of children. I made sure to direct smiles at the officer when I could. Occasionally, when the soccer ball bounced off of the chain-link border fence, he would signal us to move a bit farther away so that none of the people passing by would get hit.

Next, I decided it was time to make a more direct impression on the officer. My goal was for him to single me out to run errands, like bring him lunch, sodas, and snacks. I was going to make every effort to get closer to him. I was truly hoping that we would become friends, but I also knew that sooner or later I would betray the friendship.

After dropping some English phrases on him—How are you? Good afternoon. See you later (followed by a wave of the hand)—I took it up a notch with comments like I like your badge and Do you want me to get you something to eat?

One day he asked me in English, "What's your name?" I froze for a second because I wasn't sure he was talking to me. Then I replied, "My name is Edgar." I had no idea how I came out with this complete answer. I surprised myself. It just popped out naturally.

Then he asked me if I could get him an orange drink from across the street. He spoke in Spanish, "Quiero una bebida de naranja. You know, Jarritos." He was referring to a brand of soft drink popular in Mexico called Jarritos.

I told him, "Hablas español muy bien," which means, "You speak Spanish very well."

He replied, "Tu inglés tambien es bueno," meaning, "Your English isn't bad either."

I was surprised to hear him say that.

Also, I realized that since he spoke excellent Spanish, I was probably wasting my time trying to make friends with him using bits and pieces of English. So, I quickly responded to his request in Spanish, saying, "Si, voy por el." He handed me some change.

When I returned, a man was speaking with him, so I handed him the drink and his change. He didn't pay too much attention to me, which I was glad about. I didn't say anything because I didn't want to interrupt his conversation or get tangled up in a conversation in English.

I continued to practice my English, but I often thought, "What for? He speaks Spanish really well." But I figured that the more English I learned now, the easier my school experience would be once I was in Phoenix, if I made it there.

For us to make it the three weeks in Nogales, Miguel managed to get a temporary job at a jewelry store.

As each day passed, while Miguel was at work in the jewelry store, I was making gains with the immigration officer. I brought him lunch several times, and I thought we were slowly becoming friends.

My English instructor informed me that I was learning English at a very rapid pace, but what the teacher didn't know was how much I practiced. Words, phrases, questions, anything that came to my mind, I would repeat over and over and over and over during breakfast, lunch, dinner, walking down the streets, in the bathroom, before going to sleep, in bed.

I even practiced with American tourists in Nogales. They would shop at the many stores, looking for bargains or items not available in the USA. I talked to Americans coming to Nogales to visit dentists. I practiced and practiced without resting. Anybody that I could talk to in English, I would talk to. After a while, I thought I was becoming annoying to people, but I didn't care. I was on a mission.

> **Edgar and Miguel made a plan that would change their future. What is one plan that you could make right now that would help you achieve your big dream?**

Chapter 14

A "Quick Errand"

Finally, the day came. The plan was that I would ask the border officer a very simple question and then—assuming he said yes—I'd walk through the entry-exit gate.

My brother asked me, "Are you okay with everything we discussed so far?"

"Yes," I responded.

"Are you certain?"

"Yes, I am," I assured him.

"If it works out and you are allowed to cross, I'll be waiting for you at the Safeway grocery store. And if it doesn't work out, return to the hotel. After four hours, I'll know it didn't work, and I'll come find you there. And remember, if it doesn't go well, no one is going to harm you. He's just going to say a simple word—no."

Miguel left to wait for me on the other side. I started walking toward the gate. It was about one block away.

All at once, I noticed my heart was beating faster. I noticed my body was starting to sweat all over. My jaw became tight, like it was stuck shut, and my teeth clenched together as if they'd been wired closed.

In the short distance of a single block, my calmness morphed into full-on panic.

"Maybe they'll send me to jail. Maybe my brother won't be there. Why are we doing this? This is totally dishonest. I can't believe I'm doing this. I'm trying to deceive an honest guy. It won't work. What if they know the plan and they have Miguel under arrest somewhere?"

As I got closer to the gate, I could see the nice officer standing and talking to people crossing through the gate. He was a decent man. He had a natural smile. "Why am I doing this to this man?" I asked myself silently. "This just isn't right." I was doing everything possible not to do what I had been so sure I would have no problem doing.

I whipped around and ran back a quarter of a block. I made my way between two buildings and leaned against a building wall. My back felt wet against the dry cement. I was frightened. I wanted to run fast, but I couldn't move. I felt exhausted.

Soon I found myself in a trance, as if I were talking to my grandfather, pleading, "Abuelito, Abuelito, Abuelito, ayudame—help me!" Then I recalled something from years before:

My grandfather, a friend of his, and I were at my grandfather's farm near Playa Azul to make sure that bugs weren't eating the corn and watermelon. Towards the end of the day, right at sundown, my grandfather's friend got bitten by a venomous snake.

My grandfather turned to me, saying, "Hijo, this man is going to die if we don't get help. He's heavy, and it is impossible for us to carry him on the donkey and get him to help in time. So, Edgar, I'm going to ask you to do something. Can you run to La Mira and get some help? I'm too slow. You can run faster than me, and you can bring help. You can save him."

My grandfather continued, "I predict that you won't want to do it because you're afraid of the cemetery."

My grandfather knew that every kid feared this road because it went through a thick forest with an old cemetery in it—the same cemetery where a few years later we would bury Papá. On the way to the cemetery, trees surrounded the road, making a dark tunnel. The tree trunks were huge with big holes in them, and they were covered in snake-like vines. Abruptly the tunnel opened and graves popped up on either side, like they were filled with the newly dead, pushing to get out. The whole area had all the ingredients to make it very spooky.

He held both of my shoulders, looked me straight in the eye, and said, "Hijo, we have no choice. Can you do this?"

"Yes, Abuelito, I'll go."

I had tears in my eyes.

My grandfather stated, "What you're going to do now is you're going to run really, really fast until you get to the forest. As soon as you enter that forest, don't look to the right or to the left, and don't look back. If you do, you'll just get more scared, so don't do it. Once you reach the cemetery, stop running. That's when you walk. It will seem to take a long time, but don't run and don't look around. Just walk through it. Once you get to the other side, start running again."

I ran quickly down the road. I dashed through the tunnel of trees to the start of the cemetery. It was like a huge hole in the middle of so many trees. That's where I stopped and started walking slowly.

Walking through it, my hands were sweaty, my heart pounded, and my eyes were tearing up. I couldn't even open my mouth. My jaw was clamped shut.

To the left and the right in my peripheral vision, I could detect graves. I did not dare shift my eyes. I focused, straight as an arrow, on what lay ahead of me. I kept walking. There was only enough light for me to see right in front to my next footstep and a bit to my sides; beyond that was complete darkness.

I continued to walk slowly. My steps seemed loud. I could hear other noises too. My grandfather had told me that I would hear the crackling of the giant, hand-sized leaves as they fell to the ground. Indeed, he was right. Occasionally I felt a spurt of wind like an unwelcome slap on the back. I was tempted to look back, but I didn't.

Suddenly, ahead of me above the trees, I could see small spots of light; it was from the moon. At that, a wave of peace washed over me. I started thinking, "The moon will guide me out safely."

Once I made it through, I started running.

Finally, I met some people from the village. I started screaming that we needed help, that a man had gotten bitten by a snake on the other side of the cemetery and we needed help. The people came and helped us.

I shook my head, bringing myself back to the present. I noticed my body and mind had calmed.

I wiped my tears, cleaned my face, and headed to the entry-exit gate. All the time I kept my gaze straight ahead, not looking to the right or left or behind me. I walked at a steady pace.

As I approached the officer, I smiled at him. He looked at me briefly as he was checking someone's document.

Once I was close to him, I asked, "How are you today?"

He responded, "Great. How about you?"

"Good, thanks."

He then asked, "Would you get me lunch later on today?"

I told him, "I'd be happy to."

Then I looked him in the eye and asked, pointing to the other side, "Is it okay if I go to the store over there and buy some grapes?" I did not show any fear.

After a brief moment, he smiled. Then he gave a nod that meant yes.

I walked through the gate.

I moved slowly, not looking to the right, left, or behind me, keeping my gaze straight ahead. After a half-block I increased my pace some but maintained my straight-ahead gaze.

When I saw my brother, I smiled and wept at the same time.

> **Edgar's quick thinking helped him cross the border, but he had to lie to someone who had become a friend. Was this the right thing to do? Have you ever been dishonest to get what you wanted? How did that work out in the long run?**

Chapter 15

New Shoes, New Life

After several hours on the road, I was met with an impressive view of tall buildings and wide, black, smooth, clean streets ornamented on each side with green and red plants. It was Phoenix.

Miguel and I arrived at a two-story building whose sign read, "Silver by Lambert—Indian Jewelry." At the back of the building, several men came out to greet us.

Miguel explained to me, "These are my friends. They are the Navajo Indians that I work with."

One of the men called out to Miguel in their native language. When Miguel responded in that same tongue, I was delighted at how good he sounded.

Next a woman appeared. She had very light skin and long hair that she wore in a high ponytail. Her eyes were a green-blue, and she wore eyeglasses that had a long chain on them.

When she reached me, she said warmly, "Hi, my name is Margaret." Then she turned around and yelled, "Bernard! Come out and meet Miguel's little brother!"

A tall, white-haired, skinny man who had a thin, white beard emerged from the building and greeted me, "Hello. My name is Bernard, but everybody calls me Doc. It is so nice to meet you. I heard a lot about you."

Margaret turned to her husband, suggesting, "Let's make some hot dogs. Are you hungry, Miguel?"

Miguel admitted, "Yes, I am, thank you."

Then she turned and asked me, "Are you also hungry?"

I confirmed, "Yes, I am."

Before going inside, Margaret hugged Miguel and said, "We missed you dearly. Haven't we, Bernie?"

Bernard agreed and said one of his favorite phrases, "You bet."

Once inside, Margaret explained to me, "Edgar, this is your home. There are living quarters upstairs. You and Miguel can stay here as long as you want."

While exploring the building, I came upon a large room with many tables, around thirty or forty. Each table had its own light and something that looked like a torch.

Margaret explained, "This is the workshop and those are the work tables. You want to see the table where Miguel works from?"

She and Miguel took me over to his area. I saw a heavy, worn chair, a workbench with a drawer in its bottom, and a bunch of tools inside it as well as pieces of silver and turquoise.

Margaret told me, "Edgar, did you know that Miguel produces the finest Indian jewelry here? That's not just me saying this. The Navajos who work here say that Miguel is the most talented silversmith in the jewelry shop."

Margaret then began to talk logistics, "Miguel, when are you going to sign Edgar up for school? Fairly soon, I hope. If you can't take him to school, I will be more than happy to do that. I already told you, you can count on me for anything you need. I just need you to stay here and take care of business. We need you badly."

"Thank you, Margaret. I'm happy to be back," Miguel responded.

My first bite of a hot dog—it was scrumptious. I loved the green, zesty relish, the yellow mustard, and the red ketchup too. Also, I ate some crunchy, very thin slices of fried potato called "potato chips." I had never tasted anything like these American delights, and I loved them.

In the kitchen I studied the stove—another dream machine. I told my brother, "Mamá would certainly love to have something like this. Someday, I'm going to buy her a stove, so she doesn't have to be out there cutting wood each day to make into coals for cooking. It's hard work. It's dirty work. And then she has to breathe in all that smoke. Someday, she's going to be able to push a button and have a clean fire to cook on."

The following morning, Miguel made me soft, fluffy discs of bread with a sweet, dark sugar sauce. The food was called "pancakes," and they were delicious. It was also the first time Miguel had cooked for me. From then on, I came to realize what a great cook he was. Plus, he could make both American and Mexican foods.

It was the end of August and school would start soon, so Miguel announced, "We're going to a wonderful store to buy you shirts, pants, underwear, shoes, and socks.

Miguel and I went in his car to a big store called JCPenney. Inside it was massive, like a small village, and bright, clean, and pleasant smelling. The floors were shiny and smooth like glass. Again, it was like a dream world.

In the store, we encountered metal stairs that moved themselves upwards. I stopped and stared in wonder and confusion.

Miguel took my hand and instructed, "This is called an escalator, and it is going to carry us up to the second floor. Over there is another escalator that will carry us back down to the first floor. What you do is walk next to me. Step where I step and then stand right by me."

I loved it so much that once we reached the top, I asked, "Can I go back down on the other side and come back up on this side by myself?"

I did it three times while my brother watched with a huge grin on his face.

We walked to an area that held hundreds of pairs of pants. My brother chose a pair of Levi Strauss pants for me to try on.

I tried my best to walk out of the fitting room wearing the new pants, but it was difficult because the pants he'd chosen were huge—very long and very wide.

"Miguel, these are really big."

"You're right, but if we buy them in your correct size, by next year, you're not going to be able to wear them anymore because you'll outgrow them. However, if we buy them big right now, you'll grow right into them. We'll just give you a firm belt, and then we'll roll them up three or four times, and you'll look fantastic."

Miguel bought me two pairs of Levis, two shirts, and some blue underwear, which I had never worn before either.

"It's now time for us to take a look at shoes for you."

We approached the shoe department, and a tall lady with blue eyes greeted us, asking, "Is there something I can help you with?"

"Yes. We're here because Edgar is getting his first pair of shoes," Miguel explained.

"Well, this is a big day for Edgar then. Let's start with socks. We need to get you a pair of socks to wear when you try on shoes."

Miguel agreed, "Yes, he'll need socks."

She returned with socks, saying, "Here are three pairs. Go ahead and put this pair on."

I sat down and took off my huaraches. I pulled a sock up over one foot and then did the same on the other foot.

"How do they fit?" she asked.

I really didn't know because it was my first time wearing them, so I replied, "They fit good—I think."

"Now let's get you some shoes. Which shoes do you want?"

I pointed to a pair of very handsome brown leather shoes that I learned were called "wingtip shoes."

She brought back three pairs in different sizes. I tried them on until we found the size that seemed best.

"How do they fit?" Miguel asked.

Again, I didn't know because I'd never worn shoes before, so I explained, "They feel very uncomfortable. They feel really tight like my feet are suffocating."

Miguel recommended, "What you are going to do is start walking in them over the next few days. Then you'll break them in and they'll also break your feet in—you'll get used to each other. Then it'll feel a lot better."

With the shoes and socks on, I stood, took six steps, and then toppled to the floor. The beautiful, shiny floor made for a very slick surface to start learning to walk in shoes on!

"Oh dear. Are you okay, darling?" the saleslady called out as she and Miguel rushed over to pick me up.

"I'm okay," I replied, feeling embarrassed.

Miguel reminded her, "He's fine. He just needs a little practice walking in his first pair of shoes."

And getting "a little practice" is exactly what I did. I kept my shoes on for three days straight. I even slept with them on because I figured that the more I wore them, the faster I would get used to them, so when school started, I would be really comfortable in them and have no trouble walking.

I remember waking up in the night and then my brother woke up too. He asked me, "Why aren't you sleeping?"

I said to him, "I'm enjoying myself so much, and I'm so happy to be here. I don't know that I could ever leave this place."

Then I asked, "Miguel, what might happen because I'm here illegally?"

He told me there had been several times when he'd been at the home of Mexican friends and without warning federal agents wearing green uniforms—"La Migra"—had raided the home. Those at the house who had entered illegally would flee the scene and hide. Everyone else, like Miguel, would simply show their documents to the agents. If anyone who'd entered illegally got caught, they'd be deported back to some-where in Mexico. He said that La Migra's surprise raids could happen at restaurants, homes, on the street, at church—anywhere really. He told me I had to be prepared to run too—to run and hide and stay hidden for hours.

"I don't like telling you this because I know how scary it sounds. I hate it that I've had to put you in this position, but until we get that final paper, this is our reality. But, remember, we're going to make it right."

Edgar's new shoes represented a fresh start. Have you ever had a moment where you felt like you were starting a new chapter in your life? What made it special?

Chapter 16

A Second Language

Wearing my new clothes and shoes, I walked with Miguel to school. It was my first day.

As we walked down a hall, I noticed the floors were brown and shiny, as if they'd been polished with the same polish I used on my shoes.

The principal, Mr. McCormick, told my brother that it would be good for me to start in the fifth grade, so I could get better at speaking English. Mr. McCormick walked us to a classroom, so I could meet my first American teacher, Mrs. Tudor.

We entered a lovely room where I saw a large chalkboard and rows of elegant wooden desks with children sitting at them. It seemed there was no shortage of chairs in this school.

Mr. McCormick announced, "Boys and girls, this is Edgar. He is from Mexico. He does not speak very much English, so please make him feel welcome. I expect all of you to help him, so he can become a good student like all of you."

After that, Miguel looked at me and asked, "What are you waiting for? Go hug your new teacher."

I approached the teacher and gave her a hug. All the students laughed, and I turned to smile at them, thinking to myself, "I think I'm going to like this class."

I managed to make friends and pick up on my studies quickly. When I did not understand something, my classmates made every attempt to help me understand what was going on. I came to see them as family. Mrs. Tudor was an outstanding instructor who had only one goal in mind—to make sure that the fifth graders excelled and were totally prepared to succeed in the sixth grade. It was just as my parents had told me, "Remember that your classmates are part of your family and your teacher is your second parent."

After three months, I was able to communicate in English fairly well. In the fourth month, there were parent-teacher meetings. Because Miguel was sick, Margaret came with me.

When Margaret met Mrs. Tudor, she explained, "I'm Margaret. Here's a letter from Miguel explaining that I've been given authority to represent him in his absence."

After Margaret relationship with me was established, we proceeded with the meeting.

Mrs. Tudor explained, "In my opinion, Edgar is the hardest-working student that I have in my class—lucky for him because he needs to work harder than the rest of the students, so he can master the English language and succeed in the coming years in school."

Mrs. Tudor then handed Margaret a folded piece of paper. Margaret opened it, looked at me, looked at Mrs. Tudor, smiled, and then winked at me. Apparently my report card met her high expectations.

In just a four-month period, Margaret and I had bonded so well that I felt it would be impossible for me to be separated from her. She was like having my grandfather, godfather, and mother all rolled into one.

I went with her everywhere in her gray Studebaker. On our outings she always wore her hair up in a pony-tail tied with an elegant ribbon that matched the outfit she was wearing. She had smooth skin dotted with many freckles. She always wore bright red lipstick and carried a very large purse.

When I got sick, Margaret would bring me juice, and she fed me matzo ball chicken soup. She was nurturing, supportive, and had high expectations for me, all at the same time.

Margaret always made sure that I got all my homework done. After I completed my homework, she would review it with me, asking me one item after the other. I would answer as accurately as possible. Margaret could tell right away when my answer was insufficient or confusing. Lucky for me that was a rarity because I knew how important it was to her that I be precise.

Soon after the start of the New Year, Miguel and I were visiting some friends of his, fellow Mexicans. We were having a tasty meal of beans, rice, salsa, and corn tortillas, talking, laughing, and enjoying the coziness carried over from the Christmas and New Year's holidays.

When I heard the patio gate open, I scooted my chair over to allow the newly arriving guests—two well-dressed men—a place in the party.

Before I could settle back into the chair, men, women, and kids shot up from their seats and began charging for the door of the house or over the fence. Food, plates, forks, and knives fell to the ground as people scattered.

"*¡Tienes que irte ahora!* Get out of here and hide!" Miguel ordered me.

He repeated, "It's La Migra, so run and hide. We'll find each other later on. Go!"

I took off through the backdoor of the house and out the front, sprinting. I could hear the two men behind me, yelling, "Hold back! Hold back!"

There was a car parked by the side of the road. I ran to its far side, dropped down to lie flat on the ground, and scooted myself under it.

I could hear the two men, calling, "¡Papeles! Muéstranos tus papeles. Show us your papers!" I heard them say this about ten times.

Next it seemed they'd moved to the front yard of the house. I could hear Miguel speaking to them. They wanted to know what Miguel was doing there and what information he could give on the other people at the house. My brother told them he was only visiting acquaintances, and he only knew them by first name.

My body was trembling. I had to put all my energy towards not crying, not making a sound, not moving.

I waited at least three hours underneath the car. I didn't move once.

At one point, I figured it was safe to get out, but then I feared if I emerged too early, I would get caught: "Maybe they're hiding and waiting for the runners to feel safe and return. Then they'll capture me and I'll get sent somewhere and Miguel will have no idea where I am and I won't know either." I was in torment.

One moment everything was great—this new life with shoes and socks and school and English and

Margaret and enjoying a meal with Mexican friends in Arizona—and then I was being hunted.

Three hours later, I scooted out from underneath the car and made my way home through back alleys and in the shadows. It was late and dark.

Miguel was outside, pacing.

When I showed myself, he ran to me and held me in a big hug.

"Those were immigration officers looking to haul away people with no documents," Miguel explained.

"People like me, right?" I asked, already knowing the answer.

"Unfortunately, yes," he replied in a whisper.

Miguel had warned me that these raids happened. We knew it would happen to us; it was just a matter of when.

When the Lamberts returned from their weekend trip, Margaret could sense something had happened. I didn't have the heart to tell her, and she actually came to me, asking, "When were you going to tell me about what happened to you? You need to stay by my side. If I had taken you with me, it would never have happened. I really feel bad about it. Nothing will happen to you as long as I'm here by your side."

As time went on, I witnessed more raids and saw people I knew get hauled away before my eyes. I realized that despite her good intentions, Margaret wouldn't always be able to help me.

Four weeks later Miguel and I went to a popular Mexican restaurant. We'd just taken our seats when we heard crashing, rattling, and breaking sounds from the kitchen. It was like a bomb had detonated. Cooks, dishwashers, and waitresses escaped from the kitchen and with them waves of people from the dining area joined to form a massive herd stampeding towards the restaurant's front door.

"You know what to do. Run fast and hide and don't look back. You understand? Just run," Miguel urged.

I was already on my feet, a part of the stampede.

I noticed a man in a green outfit had his eye on me, so I ran and ran. I could see people scampering all over the place, swarming to different areas, rushing across the street, behind homes, down alleys, onto buses, over fences and walls.

I jumped a small fence two doors down from the restaurant and made my way into a neighborhood. There were at least six others doing the same. I passed several houses before making my way behind one where I found a small crevice between a wall and a water heater. Standing straight up, I could just fit in.

And so I found myself quiet, trembling, and breathing in sharp gasps. My jaw was tight. My leg muscles shook with fatigue. I didn't know whether I'd faint standing or collapse onto my knees in tears. It was agony.

But I didn't make a sound. I closed my eyes and pretended I was at the ocean with my grandfather. I waited and waited—ten, fifteen, twenty minutes passed.

Then I heard soft padding. Footsteps. The footsteps were getting closer and closer and closer.

I dared to open my eyes.

I looked up and found a man standing before me, staring at me right in the eyes. He was wearing a light green jacket with a special patch on its sleeve.

He looked at me, and I looked at him. I held his gaze without blinking.

Time seemed to stop.

Without a word, he turned and walked away.

I stumbled out of the crevice and fell to my knees. I stayed there on the ground, waiting for my body and mind to calm. I couldn't move. I could hardly breathe. I felt ill.

Later, when I found Miguel, he held me tightly, saying, "I am so sorry. I never wanted to do this. It seemed like the right decision at the time, but now it seems so wrong. It's my fault, and I am so sorry. *Lo siento, mi hijo.*"

Edgar faced terrifying moments where he had to stay strong, think quickly, and push forward despite fear and uncertainty. Even when things seemed hopeless, he didn't give up. Think about a time when you felt afraid or unsure— how did you get through it? What big dream do you have that might require courage and persistence to achieve? How can you prepare yourself now to face challenges and keep moving forward toward your dreams?

Chapter 17

Another Plan

As the months passed, I was progressing in school, and my English was getting better and better. Every afternoon I would spend about ten minutes writing a description of my day, and then Margaret would review the writing with me. After some weeks of this routine, Mrs. Tudor noticed that both my writing and speaking had greatly improved.

I also worked in the jewelry shop after school. After sweeping the entire shop, I would collect everything I'd swept in a glass jar. Mixed in with the dust and dirt were tiny silver and gold shavings. When the jewelers filed a precious metal to shape it into a piece of jewelry, these tiny flecks fell to the floor. At the end of each week, I would separate out the precious metal shavings from the dirt I'd collected. After a few months when there was a substantial amount of these shavings, Margaret would sell them and give me a small bonus.

The Lamberts kept all the precious metals, precious stones, and completed jewelry pieces in a large vault in a secured room. My other job was to make sure that all of these valuable items were in the right place and labeled correctly. Ongoing orders and incoming orders were also organized in the room. We kept everything tidy and systematized.

Only the Lamberts and I had access to this room. None of the workers, not even Miguel, ever entered the room.

When personal buyers and vendors came to place orders, pick up jewelry, or sell items, they interacted with Margaret. No one and nothing came into or went out of the jewelry store without Margaret's knowing about it. No clients dealt with anyone other than Margaret. When I was out of school and available, I worked as Margaret's "right hand man," as she explained it.

One time when I was working with her, a vendor was there to sell an item. I'd been going back and forth, in and out of the secured room, when the vendor turned to Margaret and asked, "What's the deal with the kid going in and out of the vault?"

"What do you mean?" was her reply.

"Aren't you worried about losing anything?"

Margaret stopped what she was doing and looked him straight in the eye. Next, she stated, "First of all, it is none of your business how I run this place. Second of all, Edgar is my most trusted son."

Since he'd been working with Margaret for years, the vendor replied, "No, he's not. Your son is an adult, and you don't have any other children."

Margaret paused for a few seconds and eventually replied, "Now I do. And don't you ever say anything like that again."

Puzzled, he walked away.

There was no doubt in my mind that Margaret was like a mother to me.

Miguel and I were at Pitman Foods, a specialty grocery store that had the largest array of fruits, vegetables, spices, and cooking and baking supplies of any grocery in Phoenix. We were there, searching for a certain chile, when boxes and bags went flying. Customers and employees dropped what they were doing and fled to the door. It wasn't a siege or a fire—it was an immigration raid. A huge bottleneck of people formed at the door, fighting to get out. And I was right there with them.

Though many got detained at the door, I managed to push my way out, ducking under the arms and legs of green-suited officers. I dashed down an alleyway. Then I mashed myself under a gate, crossed another street, and scooted my way through some shrubs to the back of a house. There I encountered a dog on a long chain. It immediately started barking. I hesitated, wondering if it would be beneficial to stay with the barking dog. I climbed over a chain-link fence and kept moving.

I found a house that sat on top of large cement blocks. I got down on my hands and knees, and crawled into the dark, damp space underneath. Two cats bolted out past me. I continued dog-walking it deeper and deeper underneath. I made my way past pipes, tubes, and more cement support columns. It was tight and mostly dark but with occasional lines of light coming in from the outside.

I had to keep my head low. I didn't want to go too far in because I feared scorpions and snakes, but I knew I shouldn't stay too close to the periphery either.

I felt my heart pounding. My breath was short and rapid. "This is it. This is the time. I'll never see Margaret and Miguel again. Mrs. Tudor and my classmates will find out I'm illegal, and then they'll feel angry!" my mind shouted.

I heard sounds from the outside. Louder and louder. Footsteps. Then they stopped. After several seconds I heard them again. Then they stopped.

I froze. My hands sat stiff in the cool dirt. My knees and feet also rested in a kind of paralysis. My head stayed low but cocked, so I could make out potential noises.

When I turned my head, my gaze shifted to a beam of light, and there before me, I made out a face staring straight at me. A man, also on his hands and knees, with his eyes directly on me, was positioned a few yards from me underneath the house. He was wearing the distinctive green uniform.

We stared at each other. Time seemed to stop in this eyes-locked stance. I stayed frozen.

Occasionally noises from both the outside and also the inside of the house made their way to us.

Without warning, the fear left me. Exhaustion took its place. I became so tired that I no longer cared. "I give up," a voice inside my head announced. "This is the end—so be it. He'll capture me and they'll throw me out of the country—and that's fine."

It was interesting, the way my feelings changed in an instant, from fright to not caring about anything whatsoever.

All the while, the face continued to watch me. I even detected a small smile, as if trying to coax me into trusting.

Then the man reversed his crawl, carefully moving backwards and out from underneath the house. The sound of his footsteps grew fainter and fainter. He was gone.

I burst out crying. I cried hard for only a minute and then made my exit from the dank, dark underneath. I left the backyard, jumped another fence, and made my way home.

This was the second time an agent had granted me a pass to go free. Why? What did it mean? What should I do?

Over the months since that first raid, there had been days and even weeks when I hadn't thought of raids and deportation. I could immerse myself in school and chores. But other times, when I was out with Margaret or my brother or when I was at school or the jewelry shop, I'd look around and plan my getaway in case a raid suddenly occurred. I'd become paranoid. It was a burden and a horror knowing that in a span of a few minutes my life could be turned completely around.

When I arrived home, the mood was sour. Margaret was very upset, and Miguel distraught. He hugged me, saying, "I'm sorry."

Margaret came to me and lamented, "This can't go on. You must leave. You must go and get this fixed, and let's be done with it. I will help you with everything that's needed."

We made a plan that Miguel and I would return to Nogales.

After a sleepless night, I went to school the next day. When I saw Mrs. Tudor, my eyes were slightly teary, and I felt an empty sensation throughout my body. I was about to say something when she said, "I know something is bad, Edgar. We'll talk after school."

After school Mrs. Tudor asked me, "What's on your mind?"

I told her, "It has been wonderful being here. My classmates have helped me learn a lot. I appreciate everyone, especially you, Mrs. Tudor, for all the things you have taught me."

"This sounds like a departure speech," she observed. "Is that the case?"

"Mrs. Tudor, I came here illegally. Several times now I have come very close to being deported. It's been difficult, so Miguel decided that it's time for me to return to Nogales, so I can get my legal documents. We don't know how long it will take. All I know is that I want to come back as soon as possible. Please let my classmates know why I left. Tell them the truth."

She replied, "Miguel is a good man, and he's had to make some difficult decisions for you. The fact that you're going back to straighten it out is good. Once you return, you will never be deported, and you'll no longer have to be afraid."

After spending 8½ months in the United States, I was set to return to Nogales. I was ten years old.

Edgar had to come up with another plan when things didn't go well. How do you handle it when things don't go the way you hoped? What helps you keep trying?

Chapter 18

Third Mother

W e arrived at the checkpoint in Nogales, a familiar place to me. The entry and exit gates had changed. They were more modern and looked stronger. There were no more chain-link fences. Actually, there were no gates either, only tall cage-looking sort of closets where officials were stationed. A door would open and an officer would emerge from the cage-closet space to speak to people, both pedestrians and drivers.

Sadly, during my time in Phoenix, Aurelio had died. Another man named Juan Robles had taken over Aurelio's business. Miguel and I met with him, and he gave us all the documents, including our father's death certificate, which we'd been waiting for.

All of the documents appeared to be in order, so we immediately headed over to the Consulate. We took a number from the counter and found seats. Again, we found ourselves in the big, busy waiting room. Kids were running around, and people sat nervously, waiting their turns, wondering about their futures. I just hoped that they had their documents in order and would pass legally into the US. I didn't want any of them to have to experience the terror of raids.

When our number was called, Miguel and I walked down a long hall. As we sat in a small room waiting for the Consulate official, I found myself hoping that it would not take long and that soon I could return to school in Phoenix and catch up on any lessons I'd missed.

An official entered the room, greeting us and asking that we be patient while he reviewed our documents. With all twenty-five documents in front of him, he opened my file and began examining each one, starting with my birth certificate.

After a few seconds, he asked, "Why does your last name, 'Hernández-Hernández,' on your birth certificate not reflect your father's last name, 'Hernández-Cabrera'? It doesn't make sense."

He continued, "As it stands, Edgar's last name on his birth certificate doesn't correspond to his real last name. The problem is how to differentiate Edgar Hernández from another Edgar Hernández. If Edgar's last name on his birth certificate was corrected to 'Cabrera,' it could prevent potential fraud and confusion."

My brother showed confusion. He was stunned. Then he asked, begging, "With all respect, sir, can we just go ahead and process the application, and I'll file to get it corrected at a later time? The priest who wrote the birth certificate was in his eighties when Edgar was born, and it is likely he simply made an error."

"I'm sorry, but that won't work. It needs to be done first, and then we can do the visa," the official told us.

Miguel realized he had to concede. He asked, "Would an addendum to the birth certificate be appropriate?"

"Yes, an addendum signed by the city president and by the boy's mother will work. We must have an official letter explaining the error and giving the correction. We'll go ahead and keep the application on file until you produce the required documents."

Again, it seemed I wouldn't be granted a visa due to a problem with my paperwork. Miguel and I were stunned. Shocked. Speechless and utterly disappointed.

It was a long walk back to the hotel. We paid no attention to the people around us or the vehicles that zoomed by us. We were in our own zone of stunned defeat.

Once at the hotel, my brother told me, "We're not going to give up on this. We're too far in, and we won't give up. How many of those hundred-plus people in that room do you think will be successful? And for those who find success, do you think it's easy for them? Maybe some of them will never even have a chance. But we have a good chance. Let's sleep on it, and then in the morning, we can stop by and see Mr. Robles to get his advice."

The next morning with heavy hearts we went to see Mr. Robles. Mr. Robles felt that this additional documentation correcting my last name, from a legal standpoint, wasn't necessary. But if the officer made this requirement, we had to comply. He expected the addendum to my birth certificate would take several months to a year to come through.

Once outside the office, Miguel looked me in the eye and announced, "We need to talk about what we're going to do. No matter what, I'm not going to take you illegally back to the US, and you're not going to go back to La Mira either. My idea is you'll stay here in Nogales. I'll return to Phoenix and work, and I'll come here regularly to see you. You'll stay here until we get all of the proper documents. We just need to figure out who you'll stay with here in Nogales."

We went to a restaurant to discuss ideas about who I would stay with.

After we sat down at a table and ordered food, I told Miguel, "I'm not scared at all. I'm not even scared to stay here in Nogales alone. After all we've been through in Phoenix, for some reason, I feel safe here in Nogales."

"Edgar, I appreciate your bravery. But who you'll stay with concerns me. I want you safe, comfortable, and happy. I have to feel comfortable with who you stay with. We need to find a kind person to help us. We'll find somebody. I believe we will find someone."

We had a good lunch. Our waitress was nice, with clean nails and smooth-looking hands. She had dark skin, black hair, and pretty eyes with thick eyebrows and long eyelashes.

My brother suddenly asked me, "What do you think of our waitress? Do you think we should ask her to sit with us and talk about you staying with her for a while? It's not busy right now, so maybe she has time."

When the waitress asked if we needed anything else, my brother said, "My name is Miguel, and this is my little brother, Edgar. What's your name?"

"Elvira," she replied.

"Elvira, if it's okay, I'd like to talk with you about something," Miguel said.

With a puzzled look on her face, she waited to hear what Miguel had to say.

He continued, "I know we are total strangers. However, we need your help. Edgar could not get all the documents to immigrate to the US, and I need to leave him here in Nogales because I live and work in Phoenix. Would you consider letting Edgar stay with you?"

As soon as he posed the question, she was taken aback, waving her hands back and forth as if she didn't want to have anything to do with continuing the conversation.

Miguel kept on speaking, "It will only be for a short amount of time, and we'll try not to be a burden to you."

"How long?" she ventured to ask.

"Several months to, perhaps, a year,"

"A year? That's impossible," she told him.

She looked at me and then back at Miguel. She seemed to have calmed some.

He told her that he knew he was asking for something big—and that it was hard for him to have to ask. He explained everything about our situation, even my seven-month illegal stay in the US and the fact that we had to make it right.

She said to Miguel, "I don't know what to say. It's a great responsibility to take this child with me, and I really need to talk to my husband."

My brother told her, "I'm an honest man. I have a very good job. I promise that you will be compensated. I would come back every three weeks like clockwork to visit."

"I'd like to talk to my husband. I have my break soon, and I'll return with him after the break."

Fifteen minutes later, we saw her with her husband. He was a short man with a little mustache and curly hair. They didn't come near us; they stayed over by the counter and talked for a while.

Finally, they approached us. The man inspected us thoroughly from top to bottom and then stuck out his hand, saying, "My name is Javier."

Miguel shook his hand, responding, "I'm Miguel. This is my brother, Edgar."

"How long is this going to take?" Javier asked.

"A few months to, perhaps, a year," my brother answered. "I don't know exactly. We have an attorney here by the name of Juan Robles who can attest to our honesty and good intentions. As I told your wife, I have a good job in the United States, and here are letters attesting to my financial and personal integrity. The letters are from our attempt to get Edgar a visa. This letter is from my employer."

Javier replied, "I can't read English."

"This letter says that I have a secure job, that I own my own car, and that I have a clean record with the Phoenix police department."

Next my brother took them outside to see his car. He showed them the title and registration. They talked for quite some time.

They asked, "You say you'll return here every three weeks?"

Miguel confirmed, "Yes, sir, I will be here. I will give you $100 now, and then I will pay you $20 a month. I will bring food from Phoenix too."

Elvira turned to Javier, urging, "We should help them. Besides, we have no children. He is a small child and won't take up very much room in our tiny apartment."

Miguel suggested, "Can we have breakfast, lunch, and dinner together for two days so that we can become acquainted? I think it would be good for all of us."

Javier and Elvira agreed.

Over those two days, we hit it off really well. Elvira and Javier seemed like really nice people. Elvira was warm and kind, and Javier had a laugh that was contagious. He laughed like a chipmunk.

Miguel felt confident about the arrangement.

Javier commented to Miguel, "Edgar speaks excellent English."

Miguel added, "He can write and read in English too."

Javier observed, "He could be helpful. I work at a hotel and we get many American tourists that come to do business. It would be nice to have someone that can read, write, and speak in English."

"Javier, I would love to do anything to help out," I offered.

Javier looked at me, and I smiled. We all felt pretty good about everything. So it was set—I would stay with Elvira and Javier.

Miguel drove away in his Ford Fairlane, and I walked with Javier and Elvira to their small apartment. Right after its entrance to the left of the front door, a stove was nestled in an alcove. There was a mini-refrigerator, about 24 by 24 inches. A curtain separated the kitchen area and the bedroom. Connected to the bedroom was a little closet about the size of a small kitchen table. That would be my sleeping quarters.

Elvira explained, "You will sleep in here. It's not a real mattress, but it's very spongy and comfortable, and it's warm in here."

I said, "I'm very lucky to have both of you helping me. Someday, I'll make it up to you."

Elvira gave me a hug and assured me, "You have no reason to worry. We both work, we don't have any children, and it will be great to have you here."

I thought to myself, "I am so blessed to have a third mother.

> **Edgar experiences many changes as he returns to Nogales. He also finds support from people who care about him. Think about a time when you faced a big transition. Who helped you through it? How can you use that experience to help others in the future?**

Chapter 19

Busy Little Hands

I kept very busy in Nogales. I worked at the hotel with Javier, running errands and assisting the hotel administration. I took clothes to the cleaners and shoes to get repaired or polished. I made sure people's clothing was nicely ironed and their suits had no wrinkles. I picked up meals.

At the hotel I met people from Mexico City—engineers, businesspeople that worked with textiles or home-building products, and other professionals. It made an impression on me, seeing these people coming into the hotel with their beautiful luggage and handsome suits.

I ended up working for an English teacher named Gloria twice a week. My job was to show her young pupils how to have brief conversations in English. I enjoyed working with the children. They were a lot of fun and interested in learning.

The majority of the time that I was in Nogales, I informally assisted people who were trying to immigrate. From the meetings first with Aurelio and then with Juan Robles and my two attempts at getting a visa, I'd become comfortable with the immigration process. I knew all the general requirements. I could locate the departments, agencies, health centers, and other businesses that people needed to visit to meet the various paperwork requirements. I knew where to go for the professional photos and where to go for the blood tests, skin tests, and vaccinations. I knew the most efficient and economical notaries. I also knew the reliable lawyers.

There were numerous items that needed to be done in the immigration process, and I could lead people to the experts who could help them. So, through word of mouth, individuals and families sought me out. People would say, "Go over to the hotel, and you'll find a kid named Edgar. He knows the process and the people— doctors, accountants, lawyers, clinics, agencies—he can show you around. He speaks really good English too."

Someone even told Javier that they trusted me more to lead them to the experts than they trusted the adult professionals because some professionals tried to trick people or charge a lot of money.

Sometimes the people I helped would even give me a little money. When this happened, I passed that money on to Elvira and Javier. I treated them like my parents. I wanted them to have whatever I made. I felt that I owed them that much. They were humble people.

My favorite people to assist were families with children. I loved working with children. I wanted to protect them. I remember one couple that had twin boys. They told me that for 3.5 years they had been saving money, preparing documents, and preparing themselves for immigration. They'd even sold their small home. The man was a teacher. He was hoping that he could find a better life for his children in the US. I worked with them over several months until they successfully immigrated.

I assisted people from very different backgrounds. Some people were educated. Some people were very poor. Some people seemed to have plenty of money. Other people could neither read nor write.

I found people's desires to immigrate so noble. They figured, if they crossed the border, they would make it a chain and bring other relatives across. I thought it was the most wonderful thing, hearing them explain their dreams to me. I would wake up in the morning enthusiastic about assisting these people.

Elvira, Javier, and I made it a point to have breakfast together every Saturday, so we could talk about our week and share stories. Javier was a fabulous storyteller. He loved telling stories about people that would come to the hotel. He told us about an engineer who had lost the use of his legs, so he was in a wheelchair. Apparently, this man's upper body was incredibly strong. The man had very large, broad shoulders and thick arms. His hands were huge, and his fingers were massive. The man had amazing dexterity, maneuvering himself and his wheelchair in and out of his car. It was a car made especially for him because it could be driven completely with the hands; no footwork was required. The engineer told Javier that the car had cost him a fortune.

Javier told us about wedding receptions that were held at the hotel. He described the fancy dress and radiant joy of the married couples. He described their extended families from grandparents to aunts, uncles, and little children. Javier was a person that paid attention to details.

Then, of course, he had stories about me. He explained how I'd gone to the cleaners to pick up four suits. At the cleaners I found myself deep in conversation with a guy when I was retrieving the suits off a rack. I put them on my back while I was conversing. When I reached the hotel, I handed them over to Javier, who asked, "What's this?" That's when I realized I'd picked up the wrong items—three dresses. Javier just laughed. I ran all the way back to the cleaners. When I got there, the manager was standing there, waiting for me with the four suits. He had a big smile on his face.

Every three weeks, Miguel came to Nogales to see me. He typically brought small gifts from Margaret, like t-shirts and, once, a jacket. Margaret also sent hot dogs, hot dog buns, mustard, ketchup, and relish.

Miguel brought pasta, spaghetti sauce, hamburger meat, and cheese that he cooked to make a meal for Elvira, Javier, and me. I went to the bakery to buy fresh bread. Miguel put a little bit of butter and garlic in a pan and toasted the pieces of bread in it. Elvira could make incredible desserts, and she always made something amazing, like pastel de tres leches, for our special dinners. Elvira and Javier changed into their best clothes for these meals. Javier tucked a large pillowcase into the neck of his shirt to serve as a giant napkin and protect his shirt from getting splashed by sauce.

At one of these dinners, several weeks into my time in Nogales, Miguel turned to me and asked, "You look very happy. How are you keeping busy?"

Before I had a chance to respond, Elvira answered, "You're not going to believe all the wonderful things that Edgar is doing. At first, he was helping at the hotel doing errands for Javier. On top of that, he got a job teaching English with a teacher here, and he also has been helping people immigrate. We're so proud of him—and we want you to be very proud of him too because he really helps people, especially families with little children."

With slightly teary eyes, Javier chimed in, "Miguel, we should be thanking you for allowing us to have Edgar become a part of our lives. For years, my wife and I have been working really hard, barely making it. Before, it was going to work and coming home. Now we come home and we laugh, we go to the movies, we go get ice cream, and we go out and have dinner. We really have been enjoying ourselves, and Edgar has been key in it."

Miguel replied, "Thank you, that makes me feel good."

Next, he turned to me, and we hugged. I missed him so much. I missed Margaret. I missed school. I missed everything in Phoenix. The only things I did not miss were the immigration raids. Even still, I really didn't mind the months of waiting. I had patience—and I felt like I was doing important work in Nogales.

As the months progressed, my English was getting better and better. I was also becoming much more efficient at helping people apply for immigration. Although everything was going well, there was something in particular that I felt anxious about—the immigration officer who I had tricked so many months earlier in order to cross into the US illegally. I'd promised myself that in my time in Nogales I would speak to him and apologize, but I found myself reluctant to do so. I avoided going near the area where he worked. Every time I walked that street, I would go south—away from him. I was too embarrassed to have him see me, but I promised myself, "One of these days, I'm going to go and talk to him."

> **Even as a child, Edgar worked hard to help others. What is one way you can use your skills or talents to help someone in your family or community?**

Chapter 20

Making Things Right

Around the eighth month into my stay in Nogales, I mustered the courage to speak to the border officer. At this time, it had been more than a year since I'd passed through the gate illegally.

I didn't tell Javier, Elvira, or Miguel I was going to speak to the man.

As I made my way to the gate, my heart started pounding. My legs felt slow and jelly-like. I felt my jaw tightening and my teeth chattering a bit. Everything in my body was telling me not to look for the officer.

I said to myself, "He can't arrest me, he can't hurt me, so what am I afraid of?"

I stopped and took some deep breaths. I checked in with myself and reaffirmed my commitment to tell him the truth and to apologize.

From a distance, I spotted him. He was wearing a fairly new uniform and a cap that looked military-like. He looked professional.

Upon seeing him, I started feeling good about my decision to speak to him. After he looked at the documents of two people, it was my turn.

He looked at me, and I looked at him.

He asked, "So, how are you? ¿*Cómo estás tu?* Come on in and have a seat. I've got some cold drinks."

"Thank you very much," I told him when he handed me a drink.

"Your English is great," he commented.

I laughed, and he laughed. But we didn't say anything.

Then after a moment, he asked, "What are you doing here?"

"I'd like to talk to you. Is there a time that we can talk? I don't want to bother you while you're working."

"I'll be ready to have lunch in about an hour."

"Can we meet at the restaurant across the street in an hour? I'm just going to go run a couple of errands, and then I'll be back," I told him.

He looked at me and asked, "You are coming back, aren't you?"

I laughed again, a little louder than before, and he laughed also. Here we were—laughing about that thing that had happened. I realized that this man was an incredible person. I couldn't wait to sit down and talk with him over lunch.

I went to the hotel to find Javier.

At the hotel, Javier called out, "*Hijo*, what are you doing?"

"I came over to pick up the documents that were supposed to be notarized and dropped back here for the family I'm going to meet later on."

"Yeah, they're here. They were dropped off this morning by the notary," Javier told me.

Then I asked, "Do you remember the story of when I crossed the border and I told you that I lied to the nice immigration officer? I said I was going to Safeway to get some grapes, but I never came back?"

"Yes, I remember. What about it?" Javier asked.

"I went over to visit the officer this morning."

"You did? What did he say?" Javier asked.

"He didn't say anything. We both laughed. When I left, we were still laughing. I'm going to go back and meet him for lunch soon."

"Good boy. I'm so proud of you. You're becoming a man before my eyes."

Soon after, I walked back to the restaurant to await the officer. When he entered, he had a smile on his face. As he sat down next to me, he asked, "As I recall, your name is Edgar. Am I correct?"

"Yes, Edgar Hernández. What about you—what's your name?"

"I'm Larry. Larry Murphy."

I told him, "I've been in Nogales for about eight months, and I had every intention to come and see you, but I had fears about facing you, and then finally I decided it was time. I want you to know how badly I feel because I lied to you."

"I knew you weren't coming back," he revealed.

"You did?" I asked, surprised.

He continued, "I knew it. And I don't know why I let you cross. I still, to this day, don't know why I did it. I thought about it all that day, 'What did I just do?' I went home, and I talked to my wife. I said, 'Can you believe what I did today?' The first thing she said, 'Don't you be talking about that. You could get fired.' But I told her that you would never talk about me in particular. I knew you wouldn't."

I replied, "I never did. I only described you as a nice officer, and that's about it."

"Well, thank you. So, why are you back here in Nogales?"

"I spent seven months in the United States. I went to school and had a wonderful teacher and great classmates. There's a kind lady who became like a mother to me. But there were some issues that made me come back to Nogales. I escaped several raids. God only knows why, but two different times two officers could have snatched me up and deported me—but they let me go. Now I'm back in Nogales because I want to be a legal resident of the United States. My brother and I want to make it right."

Mr. Murphy replied, "It was wrong of me to let you cross illegally. And what you're doing now—you're doing what very few people do. You returned to correct the situation. I knew you had something special going."

He continued, "Edgar, I think that we should feel good about everything, and I hope that you get your papers in line. I can tell that you'll have a great life ahead of you in America."

"Thank you for everything," I told Mr. Murphy.

Watching him leave the restaurant, I thought to myself, "What a nice, decent man. When I grow up, I want to become an adult like him—and like Miguel, Javier, my godfather, and, of course, my grandfather. Ah, my grandfather—I miss him so much."

> **Edgar wanted to make things right even when it was difficult. Why is it important to be honest and take responsibility for your actions?**

Chapter 21

Integrity

M iguel met me at the lobby of the hotel, so we could review the documents again before the appointment at the Consulate. We had the official letter that explained the naming problem on my birth certificate. The paperwork appeared to be in order. Excited, but also concerned that somehow yet another problem would show, we left to go to the Consulate.

There were five other people waiting at the Consul's office when we arrived. Miguel and I both knew that nobody was allowed to wait in that particular office until they had passed all the many requirements to get there. We knew that everybody was there for only one reason—to get the final signature from the American Consul to go to the USA with official documents.

When it was our turn, Miguel and I walked into an office to meet a tall gentleman with a flat top. He was the Consul. We all shook hands.

We sat down and the Consul started looking through the documents, one paper after another. He would look at the front, the back, and then put it back down on his desk where he would smooth his hands across it. He did this to each document.

After twenty minutes of detailed examination, he stacked the papers, put his hand on top of the pile, looked up at us, and stated, "I can't let him go across."

He was a man of few words. He looked tough in terms of his physical appearance, and his manner was stern.

Miguel looked as if he'd just been punched in the stomach.

I sat with my feet dangling off the chair. I did not know what to say or do, other than to keep still and listen. I knew something significant was about to be discussed.

Miguel asked, "But why, your honor? The papers are all perfect. They are complete. We were here several months ago, and we were told that we needed to have this final document. Now with everything complete, you're telling us that Edgar cannot go across. We have done everything right, your honor. Please, what is it that we need? What can we do?" My brother's voice trembled.

The wall behind the Consul's desk was covered in certificates—college and university degrees, military diplomas, plaques given in his honor, and even a law degree. The wall signified an impressive and educated man. It seemed like he was a man of discipline and accuracy and firm about his decisions.

He leaned back in his chair. He removed his glasses and put them on top of his desk. Then he quickly put them back on and leaned forward to state, "When I put my signature on a document to allow someone to go across to the United States, I become responsible for them. I am ultimately responsible for every individual that crosses the border, and this young child is not going across because I don't know your intentions. I don't know if you're going to make him a slave or if you're going to beat him or even something else."

Miguel responded by saying, "Your honor, I have the most noble purpose in caring for my half-brother—"

The Consul interrupted, asking, "Why aren't you caring for the rest of the children in the family too? Why only him?"

"It's a matter of finances, a matter of capabilities, sir. After bringing Edgar to Phoenix, my greatest hope is to bring the rest of his siblings and his mother across as soon as I become more financially stable. You see, your honor, I have a home that I own. I own my own car, and I am saving money—"

The Consul stopped my brother right away, "I know that. I know everything about you. You have an excellent boss. The letters here are impeccable. There's nothing wrong with the documents. I just can't let him go across because you're not his parent. You're only his half-brother."

My brother calmed himself down. Then he asked, "Your honor, may I talk to you in private?"

"Yes," he responded as he stood up, "but make it quick."

Miguel turned to me, "Why don't you step out, so I can talk privately?"

When I stepped outside the office, the secretary asked me, "Are you done?"

"No, my brother's still in there."

"You speak English well," she commented.

"I have been practicing," I told her.

"I know your name is Edgar. My name is Emily."

"It is nice to meet you, Emily," I said.

"So, Edgar, what is your dream?" she asked.

"My dream?" I asked.

"Yes, all children dream. What is your life dream?"

"You know about dreams?" I asked.

"Yes, I do," she replied. "Since I was five years old, I wanted to be a lawyer. I remember the other children in class would giggle when I spoke about representing people in legal disputes. That was my life dream. And

I achieved it. That's my law diploma hanging on the wall"—she paused to point to a framed document—"At first, I worked in administrative law, but I decided to change. Now, I get to work directly with the Consul in migration law. I love it. So what about you? What's your dream?"

"Since I was very young, I've dreamed of becoming a surgeon," I told her.

"That's wonderful," Emily replied. "So, you want to heal people?"

"Yes, I do, very much so. There's nothing more I want in this world than to be a surgeon."

"And, Edgar, no matter what difficulties you might face, don't give up on your dream. You can do it. I was the only female in my class at law school, and it was lonely and hard at times. But I didn't give up."

"Thank you for telling me this," I said. And I truly felt grateful. This conversation provided me with needed hope.

Soon thereafter, the door opened. Miguel and the Consul appeared. The Consul shook Miguel's hand, saying, "Good luck to you, Miguel." Then he turned to me and said, "Good luck to you, Edgar."

Miguel said to me, "Let's go."

Once outside, he asked, "Why don't we go across the street and buy a couple of pastries, and then we can head on home?"

"Which home?" I quietly asked.

"Phoenix," he stated with a half-smile.

Miguel drove his car into the line of vehicles set to exit Mexico and enter the USA. When our turn came, the border officer stated, "Papers."

My brother handed over a folder of documents.

The officer took the folder and headed back to his station. Ten minutes later he approached the car again. Looking towards me in the passenger's seat, he asked, "You're Edgar Hernández?"

I replied, "Yes, sir."

"Congratulations, you are now a legal resident of the United States of America."

At those words a feeling of achievement engulfed me, and a weighty burden seemed to melt from my shoulders. A great hope came over me. I wished the same glorious feelings to all the applicants enduring the immigration process.

Later, my brother explained to me what happened with the Consul. "When I asked you to step out, I knew that I had to do something and do it quick. I told him that you were my life and I could not leave without you. I also told him the truth. I told him that you and I had broken the law and that I had already taken you across illegally. I explained that I enrolled you in a school in Phoenix. I told him about the raids. I told him that we came back to Nogales to do it right and that you spent another 10.5 months in Nogales staying with a couple that we met in a restaurant who weren't even your blood relatives. After I told him this, he didn't say one word to me—for at least a whole minute. Finally, he said, 'Tell me more.'

"So I told him that I didn't mean to offend him, but I couldn't leave Nogales without you. I could hardly get these words out I was so uncomfortable about challenging him. Then I proposed a deal. I told him I'd give him my green card if he'd issue you a green card and allow you to return to the US with me. I begged him to let me live as an illegal in the US if it meant that you could be there legally. I promised him that we would return in a year, so he could see you and also read letters from your school to learn how you are doing. If he approved of the life you were living in the US, then he could return the green card to me. And he agreed."

I was speechless.

Miguel stayed silent too.

Then I thought to ask, "Miguel, without your green card, why did the border officer let you through?"

"Edgar, I wondered the same thing. I think there was a note in the documents we gave him telling him to call the Consul, who instructed him to allow me to enter."

I noticed Miguel was smiling and chuckling to himself, so I asked, "Why are you suddenly laughing?"

"Edgar, isn't it strange that you are entering with legal status—and now I'm the one who's in the US without documents? Who would've thought?"

A year later Miguel and I returned to Nogales. I had a folder of letters with me from my teachers attesting to my excellent progress.

Emily greeted us, saying, "Miguel, you look wonderful, and, Edgar, you've grown. I'm so happy to see you. It's not every day that people come back to say hello."

She continued, "He's waiting for you. Please go on in."

The Consul greeted us warmly.

I placed my binder of documents on top of his desk and took a seat.

The Consul sat at his desk, leaned back in his chair, took his glasses off, and regarded Miguel and me. Next, he leaned forward, opened the drawer, pulled out my brother's green card, and handed it over to Miguel.

At that he stood up, saying, "Good luck to you, Miguel, and good luck to you, Edgar."

"But what about the letters from my teachers and my report card?" I asked.

He replied, "I know that Miguel is a man of integrity, and you are a boy with big dreams in life. I don't need to read the letters. I already know they say great things about you. I want you to keep them. There might be a time in your life when you want to revisit them."

Miguel and I left the office and prepared for the drive back to Phoenix. At the entry-exit gate, the officer approached us. Miguel rolled the window down. "Documents please," the officer stated.

My brother pulled out his green card. I pulled out my green card. The officer reached in through the window, took the green cards, looked at them for about five seconds, and handed them back to us.

"You may pass."

> **Integrity is about doing the right thing, even when no one is watching. What does integrity mean to you, and how can you practice it in your daily life?**

Chapter 22

Scholar Days

T he coming years in Phoenix were terrific. I completed the sixth and seventh grades. Margaret and I grew closer. A few times a year Miguel and I would even go to Nogales to visit Elvira and Javier. Miguel also started the process for my siblings and mother to get green cards.

In my eighth-grade year, I was fortunate to be assigned to one of the greatest teachers ever, Francis

Cane. Mrs. Cane's philosophy was that there was no such thing as an average or below-average student. She wanted to make sure that all of us in the class were given an equal opportunity to learn, and a key part of that was teamwork. We students had the shared responsibility to help those among us that were struggling. If we were all willing to pitch in, then nobody in our class would fail. Mrs. Cane's philosophy and the way she created a strong sense of family in our classroom reminded me so much of César, my beloved teacher from La Mira.

Mrs. Cane's philosophy of teamwork worked. We were amazed at how well our classmates who had been lagging and had had poor grades and attitudes in previous years performed with Mrs. Cane. She could awaken the most reluctant or unconfident students and make them outstanding. She always said she just had to make sure that all students felt good and loved themselves so that they had confidence in themselves. After that, learning was easy.

Mrs. Cane was a person of the highest character, and she represented the true sense of the word integrity. She disapproved of laziness, gossipers, and tattletales. She disliked it if a student came to her and complained about another student. She warned us, "That is not the way you treat your classmates. Never, never do I want to hear any of you complaining to me about any of your classmates."

She demonstrated enthusiasm to us every day of the school year. Even when she was sick with the flu, had a cough, or was sneezing, she never missed work. She wanted to show us what hard work was all about, explaining, "You can't let the small things in life get you down. A cough or a sneeze shouldn't sway you from your commitments." She proved it to us herself, and we knew how strong this lady was.

She was not young either. Mrs. Cane was already in her late fifties when she was our teacher. She carried a wooden cane with a rubber sleeve on its curved handle. She had been teaching for many years. Before that, she'd been in the military.

Every year, Mrs. Cane received the "outstanding teacher" award. She was a very special person. The other teachers and school administrators applauded the recognition that our school gained due to the excellence of Francis Cane. She was adored by everyone.

Frequently her former students who were now in the high school located just a few blocks from our school would informally drop in the classroom to say hello. Mrs. Cane welcomed them and introduced them to the class. She was never put out by these unexpected visits.

As soon as they entered, Mrs. Cane would say, "Okay, ladies and gentlemen, I want you to meet one of my distinguished students who's now a sophomore in high school. She is here to visit with us for a few minutes. I want you all to say hello." Then she would ask the student, "What do you have to say to my students about high school?"

She was very blunt when asking questions. Not only that, she was famous for putting students on the spot. She explained to us that by doing that, students would develop the discipline to become quick thinkers and be able to make decisions and respond to questions in the best manner possible in a matter of seconds. She argued that it was good preparation for life.

She would tell us, "Soon, you will graduate from my class and go on to high school, and I'd be willing to bet you a penny that most of you will come back to say hello. It is among the most important moments of my life when my students come back and say hello."

Mrs. Cane's scholar days were the most memorable part of that school year. On these days, she invited certain former students who were already in college, graduate school, or pursuing their careers to speak to the class. They described their study paths and career choices. They answered our questions. And they all emphasized hard work— "If you are willing to work hard, you can achieve your goals."

On one scholar day, Mrs. Cane invited a young attorney who had been in her class many years previously. This man was extremely humble and very well mannered. He told us, "When I was in fifth, sixth, and seventh grades, I was an average student. But in eighth grade with Mrs. Cane, everything changed. The encouragement I received from my classmates and Mrs. Cane sparked a new feeling of confidence inside me. I realized I could make something out of my life. I learned to become more disciplined and responsible. I changed the direction of my life in the eighth grade."

When he was sharing this, my classmates and I found ourselves looking around at each other, as if saying with our eyes, "Aren't we so lucky to be here?"

While many students may have entered Mrs. Cane's class without thinking of their futures at all, quite soon all of her students were talking about their future careers and dreams. Students who had only had the vague goal of finishing high school, getting a job, making a few dollars, and, perhaps, marrying, transformed their dreams to something bigger. They began talking about going to college to become a teacher, a lawyer, an architect, or a scientist. They wanted to make a positive difference in their communities and the world.

Because I had realized years earlier that my dream was to become a surgeon, I was thrilled to find myself surrounded by classmates who were also thinking in terms of the big picture. It seemed all of us were thinking about the long term and about bettering the world. I wasn't alone in dreaming big—I was part of a group of peers in which it was normal. I found it ideal.

She not only opened up our minds to what we could do in the future, but we also learned the importance of generosity, kindness, and sharing. That's what the constant teamwork taught us.

Mrs. Cane actually used a cane to help her walk, and something all of us students occasionally tried to do was play a little trick on her. We'd hide her cane. Once we were preparing for an outing. We were going to take a bus and visit a museum. We were all in line, getting ready to walk out of the room, when Mrs. Cane declared, "We're not leaving until I have my cane in my right hand, and that cane better be touching my skin in a few seconds' time; otherwise, all of you will have to take a seat because we won't be going anywhere!"

Everybody began scrambling to get the cane.

Mrs. Cane turned around and announced, "I've turned around. I don't want to know who hid the cane from me. I don't care. I just want my cane back."

We were all talking, asking, "Who has the cane? Where is the cane?" Finally, it was found hidden underneath her desk. Somebody retrieved it and placed it in her hand.

After we walked out and were on the bus that's all we talked about—how respectfully she'd conducted herself with us. How she cared for us. She was not a teacher that held grudges with students. She showed equal love and affection for all students.

Eighth grade graduation was sad and special for all of us in Mrs. Cane's class. At graduation Mrs. Cane told me, "Edgar, I will never forget you. In all the years I've been teaching, I've never had a student ask as many questions as you. On a weekly basis, you ask more questions than most students ask in three months' time."

I told her, "Mrs. Cane, my teacher down in Mexico and my grandfather used to tell me the same thing. My mother warned me to be careful not to annoy people with my constant questioning."

"Every one of the questions you ask is important, Edgar, so continue to ask questions. It will make you a better student," she urged.

The next year, 1966, my mother and siblings all had green cards and were living with Miguel and me in Phoenix. In December of that year, I became a citizen of the United States of America. My mother, Miguel, Margaret, Doc (Bernard), and Mrs. Cane were all there, celebrating this landmark moment with me.

> **Edgar was excited to learn and grow. What is something you love to learn about? How can education help you reach your dreams?**

Chapter 23

Healing Hands

T his chapter takes place twenty years after my
eighth-grade graduation. I was 32 years old.

"Dr. Hernández, we need you in the emergency
room. It's a nine-year-old boy. He was in a car accident
and has several injuries. He is very ill," said the nurse.

So you see—I achieved my big dream. After high school, college, and many years of medical school, I became a surgeon. I operated on people of all ages and backgrounds to heal them. It was a challenge and a joy. I loved it.

At the nurse's request, I arrived to find a child in severe pain. The boy, Rhett, had a broken left leg, three broken ribs, and cuts to the face and arms. When Rhett told me his belly and chest hurt a lot, I did a thorough examination and a number of tests to determine he had an "acute abdomen," which means sudden and severe pain in the abdomen that is likely life-threatening. Based on my training, I knew Rhett was bleeding internally in his abdominal area. It would require immediate surgery. The problem was that I didn't know exactly where in his abdominal region the bleeding was happening. However, I had a good idea.

Before starting surgery, I went to speak to Rhett's family.

Outside, a woman ran up to me, saying, "I am Helen, Rhett's mother. How is he doing, doctor?"

I explained everything in detail that needed to be done. I told her that priority number one was to stop the bleeding in the abdomen. After that, we would work on the broken bones.

"Dr. Hernández, is he going to make it?" she asked me.

"Yes, definitely," I replied.

"Are you sure?" she asked.

"Yes, I am sure," I told her.

What I discovered during the surgery—and what I had already determined as most likely—was that one of the boy's cracked ribs had injured his spleen (a small organ that's like a tiny liver). It was his injured spleen that was bleeding. Luckily, it was only a minor injury on the surface of his spleen. I was able to control the bleeding and save the spleen. From there, another type of surgeon—an orthopedic surgeon (a surgeon who specializes in fixing broken bones)—worked on the boy's broken leg.

After the surgery, I met again with Rhett and his mother.

"Am I going to be able to play baseball again?" Rhett asked me.

"Yes, of course you are. But you must rest in bed for seven days so that your spleen can heal. After that, you'll be in a leg cast for two months. So, that's about two months off of sports, but you'll certainly be able to play baseball again," I explained.

Rhett looked at me and said, "I've wanted to be a baseball player since I was three years old."

"You can actually remember when you were three that you wanted to play baseball?" I asked.

His mother interjected, "Yes, indeed. He was three years old when he told the family he wanted to be a baseball player." From her bag, she retrieved a photo of Rhett at three years old holding a small bat.

"Do you remember taking this picture?" I asked him.

"Yes," he replied.

His mother went on to say, "All my children's dreams are to become major athletes. For Rhett, it is baseball. For the rest, it is swimming, basketball, track, and even wrestling. What about you, Dr. Hernández, did you have these kinds of dreams as a child?"

"No, I didn't dream of becoming a sports figure. When I was a child, I didn't even play sports," I told her.

Both she and Rhett had stunned looks on their faces. "What? No sports? That's so sad," she commented.

"No, it's not sad. I come from a small village in Mexico. There weren't sports there. It was an agricultural village. Most people were farmers. There wasn't even electricity. In fact, I was 9½ years old when I first saw a television and a telephone," I told them.

They looked at me with interested eyes.

"But Rhett and I aren't that different. Since I was three years old, like Rhett, I too had a big dream. I wanted to become a surgeon. Later on, at the age of nine, I knew I didn't just want to be a surgeon, but I wanted to be a surgeon in the US. I am so blessed to have had the love and support of a number of adults who helped me make my dream happen. My older half-brother, my grandfather, my mother, my godfather, my father, my teachers, as well as many others, all helped me make my dreams come true. It sounds like Rhett has that kind of love and support as well."

"Yes, Dr. Hernández, it's true. I do," Rhett told me, as he reached out for his mother's hand.

I added, "When you pursue your dreams, you are going to encounter setbacks along the way. The injuries you have right now—that's a setback. But don't let the setbacks stop you. With the love and support of your people and through your own determination, you can achieve your dreams. That's how it happened for me, and it's been a tremendous journey. I look forward to seeing what happens next, and I wish a similar wonderful adventure for you."

Edgar became a healer, just like his father. What is something you are passionate about that could one day become your career? What steps can you take now to make that dream come true?

Disclaimer

I have tried to recreate events, locales, and conversations from my memories of them. In order to maintain their anonymity, in some instances I have changed the names of individuals and places. I may have changed some identifying characteristics and details, such as physical properties, occupations, and places of residence.

Acknowledgments

I'd like to start by acknowledging and thanking everyone from my life who I mentioned already in this book. Your love, support, teaching, generosity, and enthusiasm fueled me to pursue and achieve my dreams. I am forever grateful to all of you.

I'd like to thank my grandchildren. Your very presence—watching you play and engage with the world—inspired me to write this book.

I'd like to thank my children. Writing a book takes a lot of time and effort. This is the fifth book I've written. Your belief in me and support has been instrumental to my successful and happy completion of each book. I thank you. And I'd like to offer a special thanks to my son Miguel, who suggested the very creative title to this book, which I immediately embraced.

I'd like to thank my wife, Lupe. You are an incredible wife, mother, and grandmother. It's only with your love and support that I've been able to so rigorously pursue my medical career, as well as explore my creativity in these book projects. Thank you so much.

I'd like to thank my brother Jorge. In our regular breakfast meetings, you gave me the encouragement

I needed to write this book, and your sharp memory helped supply me with vivid details from our childhood.

I'd like to thank Lori Mercer. You carefully and expertly transcribed my words from several hours of recordings.

I'd like to thank Javier and Elvira for taking such good care of me when, as a child, I found myself in need of a home and family in Nogales. You both became my family.

I'd like to thank Dr. Javier Tapia, a dentist in Mexico. You provided me with valuable old photos of Nogales from the 1950s, the time when I stayed there as a child. You had photos of the border, the hotel where Javier worked and I did odd jobs, the restaurant where Miguel and I first met Elvira, and the apartment where I lived with Elvira and Javier.

Finally, I'd like to thank Jacob Fritz. Jacob was my first friend in the United States. He took me by the hand and helped me when we were students in Mrs. Tudor's class. In remembrance of my dear friend Jacob Fritz, who recently passed.

About the Author

Edgar H. Hernández, MD, MS, FACS, lives in Tempe, Arizona, where he is a proud husband, father, and grandfather of seven granddaughters and two grandsons from the ages of four to 23.

Dr. Hernández is a surgeon at Ironwood Cancer and Research Center, a renowned oncology center in Arizona where he cares for women with minimal to devastating breast cancers. He is a diplomat of the American Board of Surgery and a fellow of the American College of Surgeons, with three times board certification. To date, he has done over 47,000 operations (and counting).

Over the course of his career, Dr. Hernández has worked with various charitable groups. He has led and participated in mission trips to Mexico to perform surgeries, teach and train Mexican surgeons, and bring medical equipment to underfunded hospitals. He's received various humanitarian awards as recognition for his service work. He's served as a keynote speaker, reminding audiences that big dreams can come true with hard work and community support.

In his free time, Dr. Hernández enjoys fishing and camping out in nature with family, something he and his grandfather did in La Mira, Mexico, when he was a child.

Dr. Hernández is the author of four other books:

- *On the Border of a Dream*
- *Miguel Hernández: Mystic*
- *Earth Angel with a Green Card*
- *In Search of a Cure*

Made in the USA
Columbia, SC
19 March 2025

55351116R00104